D1326008

THE BOOK OF CRICKET QUOTES

TEST
MATCH
SPECIAL

Dan Waddell is a journalist, novelist and author. He covered two seasons of county cricket for the *Daily Telegraph* and his books include *Who Do You Think You Are?* and *Field of Shadows: The Remarkable True Story of the English Cricket Tour of Nazi Germany, 1937*. He captains Acton 2nd XI in the Middlesex County League, where he tries and fails to pass on sage advice to young players.

Henry Blofeld has been at the heart of cricket broadcasting for over 50 years. As a regular commentator for *Test Match Special*, Blowers has brought his trademark wit, sporting knowledge and eccentric observations to cricket fans around the world.

THE BOOK OF CRICKET QUOTES

TEST
MATCH
SPECIAL

COMPILED BY
DAN WADDELL

BOOKS

1 3 5 7 9 10 8 6 4 2

BBC Books, an imprint of Ebury Publishing
20 Vauxhall Bridge Road,
London SW1V 2SA

BBC Books is part of the Penguin Random House group of companies whose
addresses can be found at global.penguinrandomhouse.com

Penguin
Random House
UK

This book is published to accompany the radio series entitled *Test Match
Special*, broadcast on BBC Radio 4 and 5 Live Sports Extra.

Head of BBC Radio Sport: Ben Gallop
Commissioning Editor: Richard Maddock
BBC Cricket Producer: Adam Mountford

First published by BBC Books in 2017

www.penguin.co.uk

A CIP catalogue record for this book is available from the British Library

ISBN 9781849909143

Typeset in India by Integra Software Services Pvt. Ltd, Pondicherry

Printed and bound in Great Britain by Clays Ltd, St Ives PLC

Penguin Random House is committed to a sustainable future for our
business, our readers and our planet. This book is made from Forest
Stewardship Council® certified paper.

MIX
Paper from
responsible sources
FSC
www.fsc.org
FSC® C018179

CONTENTS

Foreword by Henry Blofeld   1

THE BEAUTIFUL GAME   9

A BATSMAN'S GAME   27

SWINGERS, TRUNDLERS AND TWIRLERS   47

LEGENDS OF CRICKET   71

CAPTAIN, MY CAPTAIN   93

THE MEN IN WHITE COATS   105

THE BRUTAL GAME   113

SLEDGES AND SLIGHTS   137

MORE LEGENDS OF CRICKET   153

ENGLAND, THEIR ENGLAND   171

THE ASHES   195

THE GLOBAL GAME   217

THE HALLOWED TURF   231

VIEWS FROM THE BOUNDARY   239

IN MY DAY   255

YET MORE LEGENDS OF CRICKET   267

THE MODERN GAME   281

GAFFES AND GAGS   295

CLOSE OF PLAY   309

Sources   320
Acknowledgements   321
Index   322

FOREWORD
BY HENRY BLOFELD

I tip-toed into the *Test Match Special* commentary box for the first time for two one-day internationals between England and Australia, at Lord's and Edgbaston, in 1972. I had only done my first broadcast for the BBC at the end of May that year. Three months later, scared stiff, I found myself being thrown in at the deepest possible end.

For those games in the first ever international limited over series to be played anywhere in the world, a

quick look round the two commentary boxes did
nothing to help my nerves. It was like walking into
the paddock on Gold Cup day at Ascot.

John Arlott was settling in and spreading himself in
his inimitable and rather predatory way, while Brian
Johnston was busy being jocular and all things to all
men. Norman Yardley, quietly spoken, demure and
friendly; Freddie Brown, red faced, hearty and fruitily
avuncular; and Jack Fingleton, Aussie to his bootlaces
and smilingly waspish, were all welcoming. There was a
brief early morning visit from E W (Jim) Swanton, who
made an entrance I felt Bismarck would have envied.

I was going to have to work on equal terms with
all of them, which was, to say the least, scary. Alan
Gibson was in the team at Edgbaston. He was a
wonderful commentator with untidy grey hair
and a precise and teasing way of commentating.
Like Arlott, he never missed the chance to slip out
for a glass of something. Thank goodness I was
able to make common cause with another 'new
boy', Christopher Martin-Jenkins, tall, thin and
apparently much more in control than me.

Although it must have been a close run thing, I suppose I just about got away with it because the *TMS* box has remained my happy home ever since, apart from three 'naughty' years in the early nineties when I was lured away by commercial television. I was never any good at TV and soon they only used former players to commentate, so I didn't fit that particular bill either way.

I have often been asked which of the commentators I modelled myself on or tried to imitate. I would like to think that I have never consciously set out to be like anyone else. The best advice for a potential commentator is to try and be yourself. But having had the luck to work with so many brilliant performers, of course a fair amount inevitably rubs off.

Like everything in life, commentary style evolves and *TMS* today has a very different sound from when I began. While it was never exactly po-faced, in the early days it was fairly strait-laced and worked to a stricter format. Now it has become freer and more conversational, and I think more approachable and friendlier than it once was, and more humorous too.

Test Match Special today is a direct legacy of Brian Johnston who came full-time to *TMS* from BBC Television in 1970. Johnners – to give him his much-used nickname – had a natural and irrepressible humour and *TMS* was fertile ground for this. In many ways *TMS*'s reputation has come from its non-cricketing content and it is this that has made it the unique programme it has become. This is Johnners's legacy.

TMS was perhaps best defined by Robert Hudson, a former commentator himself who went on to become the Head of Radio Sport. When Peter Baxter took over at the start of his inspiring and important reign of 34 years as producer of *TMS*, Hudson said to him, 'You must never forget that for the listener, *Test Match Special* is company.' Neatly put and important to remember, for that is exactly what it is.

Of course the principal reason for *TMS* is that it should tell the constantly unfolding story of a cricket match as it actually happens. There are many listeners who, while agreeing with this, will say that the cakes and various comestibles our listeners so generously send us – and which we often talk about – are just as important. Cakes, like nicknames and many other japes, were Brian Johnston's invention. I shall offer no apology either, for birds, buses, cranes and helicopters – although maybe I should.

The other supremely important father figure for *TMS* was John Arlott. There never has been, and it is fair to say there never will be, another commentator like him. His was a combination of that extraordinary voice, the gentle poetic style, the choice of words, the implied humour and the human friendliness.

Arlott would never make a fool of a player, however much he may have fallen from grace. It was typical of the man that he felt the greatest honour ever paid to him was when he was asked to be the first president of the Professional Cricketers' Association.

Then there were Fred Trueman and Trevor Bailey, who both summarised in exactly the same way as they had played the game. On air, Trevor kept bat and pad as close together as ever he did on the field. He was always succinct and to the point. 'Can't bowl' or 'can't bat' were succulent examples. On the other hand, Fred let his hair down just as he did when he ran in to bowl: 'I can't watch this rubbish' or 'I don't know what's going off [*sic*] out there'. He had a pithy chuckle and, of course, the finest fast bowler's action in the history of the game. He was also a great raconteur about his own days as a player.

These four showed the way and helped build *TMS* into what it is today. The most important link between then and now was dear CM-J, the loveliest and most innocent of men, a supreme commentator who listeners knew they could rely on. In a lovely voice, he told it to you as it happened. He may have been the most unpunctual man in the world but so what, and his excuses were full of charming conviction.

Now the principal and quite brilliant standard bearer is Jonathan Agnew, who is as outstanding – both as commentator and interviewer – as any I have mentioned. Quite simply, Aggers is as charming as he sounds and somehow combines the traditions of Johnners and the old days with the new frontiers that the contemporary *TMS* is conquering. Another link between past and present is Vic Marks, a magnificent summariser with a naughty chuckle. He and Aggers together are as good as it gets.

Geoffrey Boycott now plays the role of the far-seeing, unforgiving Yorkshireman and he brings a sharper cutting edge to the box. His close-of-play podcasts with Aggers have given *TMS* a new dimension. Michael Vaughan is another valuable addition. Then there's Tuffers and there is no one more fun to commentate with. He is a guinea-a-minute. He knows the game brilliantly. He has a wonderful sense of humour and a near-perfect sense of timing which, on its own, is perhaps the greatest single secret of broadcasting. And to make sure Tuffers doesn't have it all his own way; Graeme Swann's pertinent, not to say trenchant, off spinner's comments are another big bonus.

For 42 years the commentators were kept in control while on the air by the amazing Bill Frindall, the Bearded Wonder, sitting in the scorer's corner.

His neat precision and accuracy were as remarkable as his copperplate handwriting. He took scoring to new boundaries before he was sadly claimed by Legionnaires' Disease in January 2009. We then moved, by way of the genial, fun-loving Malcolm Ashton, to our present scorer, South African Andrew Samson, who, beyond any doubt, is the most brilliant scorer the game of cricket can ever have known. The only downside is that he has the most execrable handwriting known to mankind.

Meanwhile, Ed Smith, Alison Mitchell, Charlie Dagnall, Ebony Rainford-Brent, Isa Guha and Dan Norcross are all rolling up their sleeves to take us on to still greater things. They are lucky to have behind them the shrewd and innovative guidance of Adam Mountford and Assistant Producer, Henry Moeran. Henry succeeded the lovely Shilpa Patel, who had shown him the way. We must also not forget the help *TMS* gets from our redoubtable Head Engineer, Brian Mack. *TMS* is surely in the safest possible hands.

THE
BEAUTIFUL
GAME

The cricket world, surely, is as crazy and inconsistent as the outside one.

Jack Fingleton

Cricket to us, like you, was more than play, it was a worship in the summer sun.

Edmund Blunden, 1944

I tend to believe that cricket is the greatest thing
God ever created on earth.

Harold Pinter, 1980

Sometimes, when I feel a little exhausted with it all
and the world's sitting heavily on my head, I pick
up a *Wisden* and read about Len Hutton's 37 in
24 minutes in Sydney in 1946.

**Harold Pinter, quoted in Lawrence Booth's *Cricket,
Lovely Cricket?*, 2008**

Dear, lovely game of cricket that can stir us
so profoundly, that can lift up our hearts and
break them, and in the end fill them with pride
and joy.

Neville Cardus, *Good Days,* **1934**

How can you tell your wife you are just popping out
to play a match and then not come back
for five days?

Rafa Benitez, Liverpool FC manager, 2005

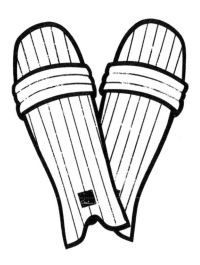

What is human life but a game of cricket?

The Duke of Dorset, *c.* 1777

Cricket never was and never can be a game of
continuous excitement or of great achievement
every day. The quiet hours, the simple strivings, are
as much part of the attraction as the unforgettable
moments of high drama. Cricket is a composite joy, a
blending of the modest and the magical.

J M Kilburn, *Cricket Decade*, 1959

What do they know of cricket who only cricket know.

C L R James, *Beyond a Boundary*, 1963

If the French noblesse had been capable of playing cricket with their peasants, their chateaux would never have been burned.

G M Trevelyan, *English Social History*, 1942

Cricket is first and foremost a dramatic spectacle. It belongs with the theatre, ballet, opera and the dance.

C L R James, *Beyond a Boundary*, 1963

The elements are cricket's presiding geniuses.

Neville Cardus

The very word 'cricket' has become a synonym for
all that is true and honest. To say 'that is not cricket'
implies something underhand, something not in
keeping with the best ideals.

Sir Pelham Warner

There is no game which calls forth so many
fine attributes, which makes so many demands
on its votaries, and, that being so, all who love
it as players, as officials or spectators must be
careful lest anything they do should do
it harm.

Sir Pelham Warner, 1932

Explaining the rules of cricket is an excellent test for high-powered brains.

John Major, former British Prime Minister

There is no cricketer worthy of the name who would not be glad to sacrifice himself if he could to win the victory for his side.

James Edward Welldon to a Japanese audience, 1906

Cricket is an ancient pastime: it ripened sweetly, it has endured nobly.

Thomas Moult, *Bat and Ball,* **1935**

If I knew I was going to die today I'd still want to hear the cricket scores.

J H Hardy

It is more than a game this cricket, it somehow holds a mirror up to English society.

Neville Cardus

Cricket, however, has more in it than mere efficiency. There is something called the spirit of cricket, which cannot be defined.

Lord Tennyson, *Sticky Wickets*, 1950

In all seriousness, [cricket] is a magnificent game which lends itself to being played (even without money) by young and old; as a game for money (not least when adults cannot play anything else) it is greatly preferable to cards, because here at least the money is laid out with very real benefits to health.

Johann Gutsmuths, 1796, in *An Eighteenth Century German View of Cricket*, 2007

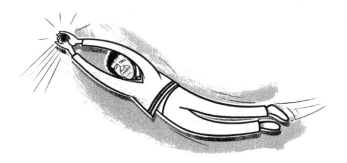

It is more than a game. It is an institution.

Thomas Hughes, *Tom Brown's Schooldays*, 1857

Cricket is battle and service and sport and art.

Douglas Jardine

Some are born with silver spoons in
their mouths. I was born in Pudsey.
You can't be luckier than that if you want
to play cricket.

Ray Illingworth

Few things are more deeply rooted in the public imagination of the English than the village cricket match. It stirs a romantic illusion about the rustic way of life, it suggests a tranquil and unchanging order in an age of bewildering flux, and it persuades a lot of townsfolk that that is where they would rather be.

Geoffrey Moorhouse, *The Best Loved Game*, 1979

Few of the great players are deep theorists on cricket, probably because the game has come to them too naturally to need any very close analysis.

E W Swanton, *Denis Compton: A Cricket Sketch*, 1948

Half the joy of cricket is playing the innings over again in your mind afterwards.

Christopher Hollis

Sex is over and done with in a few moments, unless you're Sting. Whereas a perfectly timed off-drive for four lives on in your mind for ever.

Marcus Berkmann, *Zimmer Men*, 2006

What game has survived subjection to such extraordinary manipulations, having been prolonged to 10 days (in Durban 70 years ago), truncated to as few as 60 balls (in Hong Kong every year), and remained recognisable in each instance?

Gideon Haigh

Cricket speaks in languages far beyond that of politicians.

Nelson Mandela, 1995

Cricket offers a perpetual parallel universe in which it is possible to avoid behaving like an adult until the bailiff is banging on your front door or the police have declared you a missing person.

Lawrence Booth, *Cricket, Lovely Cricket?*, 2008

It is the most English of games, complex and mysterious as Stonehenge; an acquired taste like mushy peas.

Michael Parkinson, *On Cricket*, 2002

Amateur cricket, at its lower levels at least, floats on the delusions of all of us who play. We are in love with an idea of ourselves that perhaps never existed, or if it did, it did so only fleetingly and many years ago.

Jon Hotten, *The Meaning of Cricket*, 2016

No country which has cricket as one of its national
games has yet gone communist.

Woodrow Wyatt

There are many of us, and we are all the same ...
we stumble cheerfully through life, performing
normal tasks and living relatively normal lives,
while at the back of our minds a small but
insistent question lurks. What's the Test score?

Marcus Berkmann, *Rain Men*, 1995

There is no such thing as a crisis in cricket,
only the next ball.

W G Grace

The mere mention of the words 'village' and
'cricket' conjures up a sepia-toned rustic idyll, full
of burly blacksmiths and wily off-spinning
parsons and chaps called Jack with pipes,
who always score a hundred in even time
but never hit across the line.

Marcus Berkmann, *Rain Men*, 1995

Cricket records, like Aunt Sallies, exist primarily to be knocked down. In part this accounts for the optimism with which most cricketers are endowed when facing long odds.

Douglas Jardine, 1937

Cricket civilises people and creates good gentlemen. I want everyone to play cricket in Zimbabwe; I want us to be a nation of gentlemen.

Robert Mugabe, 1984

But after all it's not the winning that matters, is it? Or is it? It's – to coin a word – the amenities that count; the smell of the dandelions, the puff of the pipe, the click of the bat, the rain on the neck, the chill down the spine, the slow exquisite coming on of sunset and dinner and rheumatism.

Alistair Cooke (no, not that one)

Cricket is like sex films. They relieve frustration and tension.

Linda Lovelace, American adult movie actress, who obviously had never seen England bat

I suppose doing a love scene with Raquel Welch roughly corresponds to scoring a century before lunch.

Oliver Reed

Basically it's just a whole bunch of blokes standing around scratching themselves.

Australian author Kathy Lette

A
BATSMAN'S
GAME

Given the choice between Raquel Welch and a
hundred at Lord's, I'd take the hundred.

Geoff Boycott, 1981

Find out where the ball is.
Go there. Hit it.

**KS Ranjitsinhji outlines the eternal truths
of batsmanship**

Batsmen are the darlings of the committees; bowlers
are cricket's labourers.

**Don Bradman on another of the game's
eternal truths**

Cricket is a batsman's game. The city of London has never emptied to watch a bowler as it did Bradman.

E W Swanton

Nerves play as important a part in batsmanship as skill.

Gilbert Jessop

In the eyes of any true cricket lover it is possible for an innings of 10 runs to be better (i.e. more elegant) than an innings of 100 runs.

George Orwell, with a sentence to make any Yorkshireman's blood boil

I don't know, lad. It's unplayable at my end, but they're bowling bloody rubbish to you.

Brian Close, captain of Somerset, to a young Peter Roebuck

A natural mistimer of the ball

**Angus Fraser on Mike Atherton (as quoted
by Atherton himself in 1996)**

Hick is just a flat track bully.

John Bracewell on Graeme Hick, 1991/92 tour

A bank clerk going to war.

***The Sun* on David Steele, 1975 Ashes**

A corpse with pads on.

An English journalist on Bill Lawry, 1968 Ashes

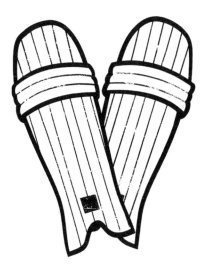

I never wanted to make a hundred. Who wants to make a hundred anyway? When I first went in, my immediate objective was to hit the ball to all four corners of the field. After that I tried not to be repetitive.

Learie Constantine, 1963

I couldn't bat for the length of time required to score 500. I'd get bored and fall over.

Denis Compton, 1994

Batting is a major trial before an 11-man jury.

Richie Benaud

His batsmanship should have been weighted in carats, not runs.

Ray Robinson on stylish Aussie batsman A F Kippax,
***Between Wickets*, 1946**

Colin Milburn is as untidy as an unmade bed, as devastating as a hand grenade.

Clive Taylor

I don't have the patience for [golf]. It's a long way to walk before you have a pint ...

Colin Milburn

The cut was never a business stroke.

Wilfred Rhodes

He [Denis Compton] played so late that his stroke was within a sparrow's blink of being posthumous.

John Arlott, 1948

[Dexter] seems to find time to play the fastest of bowling, and still retain dignity, something near majesty as he does it.

John Arlott, 1963

His bat has as many holes in it as a Henry Moore sculpture.

John Arlott

He's not a man, in general, over-afflicted with patience in his batting.

John Arlott on Rohan Kanhai, 1966

The stroke of a man knocking a thistle top off with a walking stick.

John Arlott on Clive Lloyd, World Cup Final, 1975

Never cut or pull until the chrysanthemums have
flowered.

Batting advice passed to Michael Parkinson from his father

It's hard work making batting look effortless.

David Gower, 1989

I don't believe in technique, I believe in performance.
If you are tough, whether you have technique or not,
you will survive.

Virender Sehwag

No good hitting me there mate, nothing to damage.

Derek Randall to Dennis Lillee after the latter hit him on the head in the 1977 centenary test in Melbourne

Dear Mum, things are looking up. Today I got a half volley in the nets ...

David Lloyd in a letter home from the 1973/74 Ashes, where England were trounced by Lillee and Thomson

Cricket is a most precarious profession; it is called a team game but, in fact, no one is so lonely as a batsman facing a bowler supported by ten fieldsmen and observed by two umpires to ensure that his error does not go unpunished.

John Arlott, *An Eye for Cricket*, 1979

Come and look at this. You've never seen anything like it.

Don Bradman urges his teammates to watch Stan McCabe score 127 runs in a session at Trent Bridge in 1938, which he considered the greatest innings ever played

My eyes were filled as I drank in the glory of his shots.

Ibid

I should like to say that good batsman are born, not made; but my long experience comes up before me, and tells me that it is not so.

W G Grace

I can't really say I'm batting badly. I'm not batting long enough to be batting badly.

Greg Chappell's assessment of a poor run of scores

Just bloody go after him, mate, and see what happens.

Doug Walters after being asked how he'd counter the wiles of Abdul Qadir

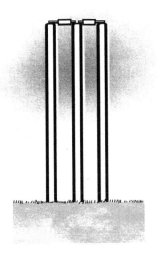

Some people don't believe in form.
Just one good shot away from getting it
all back, they say. I do believe in it. I know
what it feels like to stand at the crease
full of confidence, with stacks of runs
under my belt. I also know … the quiet
turmoil of bad form. Please God, give
me a start, just a start, and I will be
all right.

Ed Smith, *On and Off the Field*, 2005

Before my time it was considered rather *infra dig* to
hook a ball round to the leg side. Nowadays
batsmen will step right across and hook
from wide of the off stump round to square leg.
Hammond is the great exception. He won't
hook … But then Hammond, as a batsman,
is a law unto himself.

Jack Hobbs, *Wisden*, 1935

This thing can be done.

Fred Spofforth to fellow bowler George Giffen, faced with England needing to score 85 to beat Australia in 1882

Nice night for it, then?

Yorkshire and England all-rounder Graeme Stevenson to Ian Chappell on his way to bat for England in a day-nighter against Australia, with the game in the balance, 1980

Y'know, we can piss this, chum.

Fellow Tyke David Bairstow to Stevenson when he got to the wicket

England won with an over to spare and they strolled in like they'd been taking their dog for his evening walk.

Frank Keating after Stevenson and Bairstow had won the game, *Another Bloody Day in Paradise!*, 1981

Gower spoke: 'What the heck am I doing wrong,
Fiery?' he asked Sir Geoffrey.
'Nothing,' said Boycott, 'that were a very good
innings till you threw it away. You've got to steel
yourself to concentrate every ball – *for England* –
you've got to go out there and bat all day *for England!*
It's not a county match out there, y'know.'

**As recorded by Frank Keating in *Another Bloody Day in
Paradise!*, 1981**

It's very rewarding being a pain in the arse.

**Jack Russell after his and Michael Atherton's rear-guard
displays saved the Johannesburg Test in 1995 for England**

I still have the butterflies, but now I have them in
flying formation.

**Australian batsman and captain Mark Taylor, enduring a
run of bad form**

When I'm batting I like to pretend I'm a West Indian.

Darren Gough

Test cricket is bloody hard work, especially when you've got Sachin [Tendulkar] batting with what looks like a three-metre-wide bat.

Mike Hussey

We know you can lose wickets in clusters and we
seem to have lost 10 there in a cluster.

Alastair Cook, 2010

There are elements of others, including
Gilchrist and Miandad, but Warner has
unconsciously put them together to make
a unique and compelling character: a
gloriously talented troll who leaves
opposing players and fans foaming
with impotent rage.

Rob Smyth on David Warner, 2014

Much as I admire the man I've been named after, my
fellow Yorkshireman Geoffrey Boycott, I'm not all
that keen on being compared to him for my running
between the wickets.

Joe Root muses on his new nickname, 'Geoffrey', 2015

For a large part of that I thought, there is no way I
get paid enough to be facing him. And I do alright
for myself, don't get me wrong.

Rob Key on facing the pace of Mitchell Johnson, 2015

You've only got to last two balls and then
you'll be fine.

**Jimmy Cook, dismissed for a golden duck on his Test
debut, gives advice to his son Stephen before his first Test
match**

SWINGERS,
TRUNDLERS
AND TWIRLERS

To be a great fast bowler, you need a big heart and a big backside.

Fred Trueman, who had both

Down the mine I dreamed of cricket; I bowled imaginary balls in the dark; I sent the stumps spinning and heard them rattling in the tunnels. No mishap was going to stop me from bowling in the real game, especially this one.

Harold Larwood

Eeyore without the *joie de vivre*

Mike Selvey on Angus Fraser, 1996

I look like I do on the field because what I do is
knackering.

Angus Fraser

A 1914 biplane tied up with elastic bands vainly
trying to take off.

Frank Keating on Bob Willis

Emmott cherished the new ball clearly; he would carry it between overs in person to the next bowler needing it after himself; and he would contain it in the palms of his hands like a sacred chalice.

Neville Cardus on Emmott Robinson

You guys are history ...

Devon Malcolm to the South African team, having been struck by a bouncer, 1994. He went on to take a matchwinning 9–57.

Sorry Godfrey but I have to do it – the crowd are a bit bored at the moment.

Keith Miller to Godfrey Evans after bowling two bouncers at him in 1946/47 Ashes

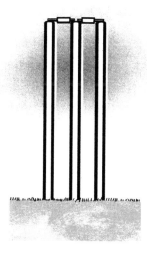

No bugger ever got all ten when I was at
the other end.

**The great S F Barnes reflecting on Laker's
feat v Australia**

A fag, a cough, a cup of coffee.

**Brian Statham on his pre-match routine,
as told by Frank Tyson**

You don't need a helmet facing Waqar so much
as a steel toe-cap.

Simon Hughes on Waqar Younis' lethal yorkers

There's not a batsman on earth who goes out to face
Lillee and Thomson with a smile on his face.

Clive Lloyd, 1975

I was once timed at 99.97 mph, but that's
rubbish – I was miles faster than that.

Jeff Thomson

I enjoy hitting a batsman more than getting him out.
I like to see blood on the pitch.

Jeff Thomson, 1974

I kept smiling at Thomson, hoping to keep him in a
good mood.

**Sri Lankan batsman Ranjit Fernando, who saw two of his
teammates forced to retire hurt by Thomson in the 1975
World Cup**

Consider Lillee in the field. He toils, but does not spin.

John Arlott

I don't know why they bother to put the stumps out.
None of those buggers are trying to hit them.

Graeme Fowler on the 1985 West Indies pace quartet

Fast bowlers are bully boys. They dish it out but they can't take it.

Brian Close

There's no sitting duck like a scared duck.

Ray Lindwall

When Ian Botham tried one at Taunton, you could unfailingly spot it from Yeovil.

Frank Keating on Ian Botham's slower ball

Bowlers, in the future as in the past, will be
applauded and rewarded far less than batsmen.

Phil Edmonds, 1989

To bowl fast is to revel in the glad animal action,
to thrill in physical power and to enjoy a certain
sneaking feeling of superiority over mortals who play
the game.

Frank Tyson, *A Typhoon Called Tyson*, 1961

The value of a good bowler is often overlooked by
some spectators, and his success is attributed too
readily to bad batting.

Hedley Verity, *Bowling 'em Out*, 1936

What, are you going, Doctor? There's still one stump standing.

Charles Kortright to W G Grace after
bowling him

I don't suppose I can call you a lucky bleeder
when you've got 347.

**Angus Fraser to Brian Lara during his record-
breaking 375 in 1994**

Facing a fast bowler is like standing on the outside
lane of the M1, and when the car is 22 yards away,
trying to get out of the way.

Alec Stewart

None of us likes fast bowling, but some of us don't
let on.

Maurice Leyland

What we have here is a clear case of Mann's
inhumanity to Mann.

**John Arlott, when George Mann was bowled by his
namesake Tufty Mann, 1947**

Loader is jumping all over the place like a monkey
on a stick.

**John Arlott after Peter Loader got a hat-trick against the
West Indies, 1957**

He reminds me of Groucho Marx chasing a pretty
waitress.

**John Arlott on Pakistan's Asif Masood's distinctive
run-up, 1971**

Wickets are more important than waistline.

Merv Hughes

The mincing run-up resembles someone in high heels and a panty girdle chasing a bus.

Martin Johnson on Merv Hughes

An ordinary bloke trying to make good without ever losing the air of a fellow with a hangover.

Roebuck on Merv Hughes, 1988

I just try to bore the batsman out. It's pretty simple stuff but the complicated thing is to keep it simple.

Glen McGrath

Get a single down the other end and let
someone else play him.

Geoff Boycott on how to play Glen McGrath

England went in and Holding bowled
the most lethal, most frighteningly
enthralling, over to Boycott that any
sadist could wish to witness. The first ball was
gentle, the second less so, the third, fourth
and fifth increasingly made one fear for
Sir Geoffrey's gallant life and the sixth – as
though the hateful half-dozen had been
orchestrated into one gigantic crescendo – tore
the stump from the ground and had it
spearing for some twenty yards as if for the very
heart of wicketkeeper Murray.

**Frank Keating on what some consider to be the finest
and fiercest over ever bowled, *Another Bloody Day in
Paradise!*, 1981**

For one hour, on an untrustworthy pitch, he bowled
like the very devil himself.

**Mark Nicholas on Curtly Ambrose's spell of 6–24, which
bowled England out for 46 in 1994**

There is something reminiscent of a wild animal
in the sight of Kapil Dev on the cricket field. He
is a restless figure, erect and alert, saucer eyes
darting hither and thither, muscles, it seems,
twitching like a deer on the lookout for danger.

Christopher Martin-Jenkins, *Cricket Characters*, 1987

It's like having a superpower – it's a surge, an urge.

**England paceman Simon Jones
on bowling fast**

Peter Siddle's first Test wicket.

**Peter Siddle shows his quick wit when
asked how he would describe
Sachin Tendulkar, 2012**

There's nothing wrong with being aggressive –
the bloke down the other end has a bat,
some pads and a helmet.

Simon Jones

I just close my eyes and wang it down.

Matthew Hoggard gives away the secret of his success

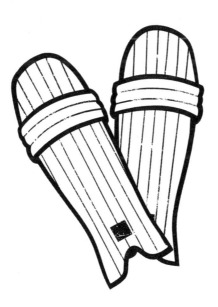

And my tip to all bowlers – learn to bat! Bowling is for mugs.

Kevin Pietersen's advice to county bowlers, 2012

It's unrealistic to get your yorkers going bowling with a bar of soap.

Stuart Broad on the struggles of bowling with a dew-soaked ball during the World T20 match against South Africa, 2014

If a batsman thinks it's spinning, it's spinning.

Wilfred Rhodes

I'm alright when his arm comes over, but I'm out of form by the time the bloody ball gets there.

Fred Trueman on the looping spin of Peter Sainsbury

The face of a choirboy, the demeanour
of a civil servant and the ruthlessness of
a rat-catcher.

Geoff Boycott on Derek Underwood

There was a time when a batsman had more chance
of being hit by space debris than being done in the
flight by Ashley Giles.

Mike Selvey

Mentally, my stock ball pitches leg and hits off.

Phil Edmonds, *A Singular Man,* **1986**

When you're an off-spinner, there's not much point glaring at batsmen. If I glared at Viv Richards he'd just hit me further.

David Acfield, 1982

How anyone can spin the ball the width of Gatting boggles the mind.

**Martin Johnson on the 'ball of the century' by
Shane Warne to Mike Gatting, 1993**

Part of the art of bowling spin is to make the batsman think something special is happening when it isn't.

Shane Warne

No cricketer is so dependent on the turf on which the game is played as the spinner; it can make, break, enfang or defang him.

Gideon Haigh

You can't smoke 20 a day and bowl fast.

Phil Tufnell, 1990

The other advantage England have got when
Phil Tufnell is bowling is that he isn't fielding.

Ian Chappell, 1990/91 Ashes

All have to do is bowl loopy-doopies to them and
they commit suicide.

**Tufnell gives valuable insight into his success against the
West Indies in 1994**

Bowling has the problem of wildly differing methods
so that placing Wasim Akram against Bishan Bedi
is rather like hanging a Rembrandt next to a Picasso
and trying to produce a valid comparison.

Patrick Ferriday, ***Masterly Batting,*** **2013**

Some are born medium-paced, some become medium
paced and others have medium pace thrust upon them.

Harry Pearson, ***The Trundlers,*** **2013**

At one end I felt like Donald Bradman,
at the other Donald Duck.

**Ray East on scoring 48 against a Hampshire side
boasting Malcolm Marshall**

When Bishan Bedi bowled, every day seemed bathed
in sunshine.

Patrick Murphy, *The Spinner's Turn*, 1982

LEGENDS
OF
CRICKET

In play, the salient feature of his cricket
was that it seemed so unspectacular:
he batted perfectly because he was the
perfect batsman.

John Arlott on Jack Hobbs, *Book of Cricketers*, 1979

He could have made 400 centuries – and
if he'd played for Yorkshire he would
have done.

Wilfred Rhodes on Jack Hobbs

He was the great arch or bridge over which
cricket of the Golden Age strode into the
twentieth century.

Neville Cardus on Jack Hobbs, 1952

A snick by Jack Hobbs is a sort of disturbance of cosmic orderliness.

Neville Cardus

Grace, then, is the Beethoven of cricket, bridging the old game and the modern just as Beethoven bridged the classical and the romantic in music.

Gerry Cotter, *The Ashes Captains*, 1989

He revolutionised cricket. He turned it from an accomplishment into a science.

K S Ranjitsinhji on W G Grace, *The Jubilee Book of Cricket*, 1897

Arguably, cricket and Grace died together.

Eric Midwinter, *W G Grace*, 1981

He was as modest as he was magnificent: batting
seemed to be just part of himself.

Pelham Warner on Victor Trumper,
***Barclays World of Cricket*, 1986**

Victor Trumper had the greatest charm and two
strokes for every ball.

C B Fry

Like all the best bowling craftsmen he hated
batsmen and believed that every ball delivered
should be their last.

Bernard Hollowood on the legendary Sydney Barnes,
***Cricket Brain*, 1970**

Barnes scythed through batsmen because he believed in the divine right of Barnes.

Ibid

When George Hirst got you out, you
were out. When Wilfred got you out,
you were out twice, because he knew by
then how to get you out in the
second innings.

Roy Kilner on the genius of Wilfred Rhodes

Great batting often has the beauty of the blast or
the grandeur of the gale. In Headley's art there is no
poise. But it answers the test of greatness. As he walks
down the pavilion steps you expect, in hope or fear.
Only three or four men can do this for you always.

R C Robertson-Glasgow on George Headley

Easy to watch, difficult to bowl to, and impossible to write about. When you bowled to him, there weren't enough fielders; when you wrote about him, there weren't enough words.

R C Robertson-Glasgow on Frank Woolley

As I ran up, Bradman seemed to know what I was going to bowl, where the ball was going to pitch, and how many runs he was going to score.

Jim Laker on Don Bradman

Bradman was the summing up of the Efficient Age which succeeded The Golden Age. Here was brilliance safe and sure, streamlined and without impulse. Victor Trumper was the flying bird; Bradman the aeroplane.

Neville Cardus, *Autobiography*, 1947

A number of Bradmans would soon put an end to the glorious uncertainty of cricket.

Neville Cardus

He had all the strokes – and the will and the nerve to crush a bowler's heart.

Alec Bedser on Bradman

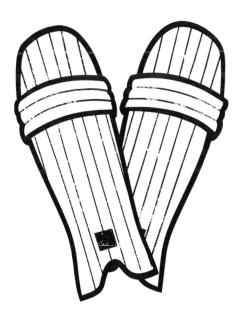

They said I was a killer with the ball without
taking into account that Bradman with a bat
was the greatest killer of all.

Harold Larwood on Bradman

I think the Don was too good: he spoilt the game ...
I do not think we want to see another like him. I do
not think we ever shall.

Jack Hobbs on Bradman

The one person who came close to mastering the game.

Keith Stackpole on Bradman

Don Bradman will bat no more against England, and two contrary feelings dispute within us: relief, that our bowlers will no longer be oppressed by this phenomenon; regret, that a miracle has been removed from among us. So must ancient Italy have felt when she heard of the death of Hannibal.

R C Robertson-Glasgow, 1948

He is a text-book of batting come to life with never a
misprint or erratum.

J M Kilburn on Bradman

Whenever he hit the stumps a broad smile came
across his face which he tried to conceal. It would
not interest him if somebody was caught off his
bowling.

**Arthur Carr on his Nottinghamshire teammate
Harold Larwood**

This man thought a full toss was the worst form of
cricket vandalism and the long hop a legacy from
prehistoric days when barbarians rolled boulders
towards the enemy.

**Arthur Mailey on Clarrie Grimmett, *10 for 66
and All That*, 1958**

He was one of the last of his kind – and certainly
the finest specimen of it – the amateurs, the smiling
gentlemen of games, intensely devoted to the skill
and the struggle but always with a certain gaiety,
romantic at heart but classical in style.

J B Priestley on C B Fry, *The English*, 1973

Hitler might have died of a fit trying
to get a word in.

**Neville Cardus ruing the fact that C B Fry did not speak
German in his meeting with Hitler, 1934**

Grandeur was his cloak and gratitude for it must be his memorial.

J M Kilburn on Wally Hammond, *Cricket: The Great Ones*, 1967

His place in the Permanent National Gallery of Cricketers is safe – not as a painting but as a nobly looming sculpture.

Neville Cardus on Wally Hammond, *Barclays World Of Cricket*, 1986

For Hammond was majesty and power; Hammond was grace, beauty and courage. One glorious cover-drive from him and I would be content.

Margaret Hughes, *All on a Summer's Day*, 1953

Whenever I saw Wally Hammond batting, I felt sorry for the ball.

Leonard Hutton

I'm only setting up these records for Hutton to break them.

Herbert Sutcliffe on Leonard Hutton

Hutton was never dull. His bat was part of his nervous system. His play was sculptured. His forward defensive stroke was a complete statement.

Harold Pinter, *Hutton and the Past in Cricket '72*, 1972

He was Horatius on the tottering bridge; Hector, who alone stood between Troy and destruction. He was born to rescue.

R C Robertson-Glasgow on Maurice Leyland, *Cricket Prints*, 1943

Already they are like kings; benevolent kings appointed and acclaimed by like-minded subjects; champions in the fight against dullness and the commercial standard.

R C Robertson-Glasgow on Compton and Edrich in the glorious summer of 1947

[Denis] Compton was so joyously haphazard that
John Warr remarked that his call was merely an
opening bid.

I A R Peebles and Diana Rait Kerr, *Lords 1946–1970*, 1971

Greatness was in him and it was not obscured.

**J M Kilburn on Fred Trueman, *A History of Yorkshire
Cricket*, 1970**

If anyone beats
it, they'll be
bloody tired.

**Fred Trueman on getting the record for most
Test wickets, 1964**

Tell me Fred, have you ever bowled a
ball which merely went straight?

Richard Hutton to teammate Fred Trueman

Neil Harvey always had sunlight gleaming across his
cricket.

David Frith, *Cricket Heroes*, 1985

He offered the cricket of lyric and freedom; the joy of
those whose forefathers had shed the bondage of slavery.

**Gerald Howat on Learie Constantine, *Cricket's Second
Golden Age*, 1989**

I would have died for Yorkshire. I suppose once or twice I nearly did.

Brian Close

And still Close has not rubbed any part of him. What an amazing man he is ...

Henry Blofeld marvels at the bravery of 45-year-old Brian Close, facing up to a fast bowling battery from Michael Holding in 1976

To describe Sobers' method I would use the term lyrical. His immense power is concealed, or lightened, to the spectator's eye, by a rhythm which has in it as little obvious propulsion as a movement of music by Mozart.

Neville Cardus, *Wisden*, 1967

I suppose I can gain some consolation from the fact that my name will be permanently in the record books.

Malcolm Nash on being hit for six sixes in an over by Sobers in 1968

You're the 12th journalist to contact me this week. Yes, I get frustrated. It's been talked about for 40 years. There really is nothing else to add.

Malcolm Nash realises that being in the record books is not all it's cracked up to be

It was not sheer slogging through strength, but scientific hitting with every movement working in harmony.

Tony Lewis, on Sobers' six sixes

On the field with him you sense that he knows every blade of grass by name.

Tony Lewis on Ray Illingworth

He crept and shuffled rather than bobbed up to the bowling crease, ball held sinisterly, as if it were a grenade he was about to lob into an enemy trench. Here was wisdom of the hard Northern kind.

David Frith on Ray Illingworth, *The Slow Men*, 1984

I didn't see Peter May, but even Ray Illingworth said he was tremendous. For him to say that about somebody with three initials who had a southern background and went to public school, he must have been good.

Michael Atherton on Peter May, 1997

In an age preoccupied by accountancy, he has given the game warmth and colour and inspiration far beyond the tally of the scorebook.

J M Kilburn celebrates the brilliance of Tom Graveney

The batsmanship of Our Tom, was of the orchard rather than the forest, blossom susceptible to frost but breathing in the sunshine.

Frank Keating does likewise in 2003

In cricketing terms Graeme Pollock is a sadist.

Eddie Barlow on fellow South African Pollock

CAPTAIN,
MY
CAPTAIN

Captaincy is ninety per cent luck and
ten per cent skill. But don't try it without
the ten per cent.

Richie Benaud

As captain you can never be one of the boys.

Tony Lewis, *Playing Days*, 1985

Cricket teams have often suffered from captains who have arrived, done queer things, departed and been forgotten.

R C Robertson-Glasgow, *Cricket Prints*, 1943

Captaincy seems to involve half-hearing conversations which you'd rather not hear at all.

Peter Roebuck, *It Never Rains*, 1984

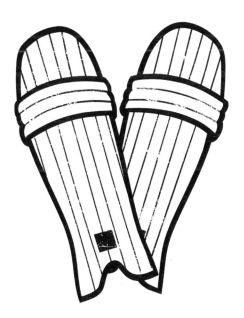

Pray God, no professional shall ever captain England.

Lord Hawke, 1925

Amateurs have always made, and always will make,
the best captains, and this is only natural.

Allan Gibson 'A G' Steel, former England captain

One word sums up a successful cricket captain:
versatile. He needs the patience of a saint, the
diplomacy of an ambassador, the compassion of a
social worker, and the skin of a rhino.

Ray Illingworth, *Captaincy*, 1980

A captain cannot make a bad side into a good one,
but a great side can make an indifferent captain into
a moderate one.

Douglas Jardine, 1933

It is easier for a football manager to 'play God,'
to read the riot act to players, because he does
not have to perform himself. Sales managers
don't sell, foremen don't hump bricks. All
cricket captains bat and field, and some bowl.
We receive repeated intimations of our own
mortality.

Mike Brearley, *The Art of Captaincy*, 1985

May, I should say, is a cavalier batsman
and a roundhead captain.

A A Thomson, *Hirst and Rhodes*, 1959

Captaincy by committee on or off the field is lamentable.

A E Knight, *The Complete Cricketer*, 1906

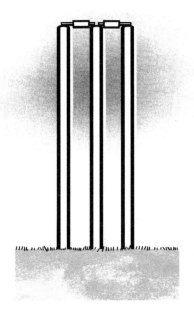

I have heard some English captains speak
to their professionals like dogs.

Joe Darling, 1902

They can all resign themselves to the fact that
none of them will ever be as good as the talkative
gentleman with the packet of ham sandwiches who
sits square with the wicket on every county ground
in the land.

Doug Insole on the life of the county captain

There's only one captain of a side when
I'm bowling – me.

Sydney Barnes

One of you bugger off and the rest scatter.

**Keith Miller reportedly, while captaining
New South Wales**

What you get from Nasser is honesty. There aren't many captains who look you in the eye and tell you you're a tosser.

Darren Gough on life under Nasser Hussain

You do have a private income, don't you?

**Unnamed Middlesex committee member
to Mike Brearley after his appointment as captain**

When I win the toss on a good pitch, I bat. When I win the toss on a doubtful pitch, I think about it a bit and then I bat. When I win the toss on a very bad pitch, I think about it a bit longer, and then I bat.

W G Grace

Try to win in two days. If you can't, lose in two days, so we can have a day off.

Colin Ingleby-Mackenzie

A captain's job nevertheless, is bound up with the aim of removing batsmen by any fair means at his disposal, and there is certainly some psychology involved in this.

Keith Fletcher

He stood in the gully cackling at Gooch's
jokes while he plotted each batsman's downfall.
It's very disconcerting if you're that
batsman.

Simon Hughes on the genius of Keith Fletcher, *A Lot of
Hard Yakka*, **1998**

You'll have the most miserable time of your life.

**Brian Close, somewhat prophetically, to Ian Botham after
he was made England captain in 1980**

At one stage Hogg suggested we survey the back of
the Adelaide Oval – and I don't think he had tennis
in mind.

**Graham Yallop, captain of Australia, on his tempestuous
relationship with fast bowler Rodney Hogg**

Now lads, I don't want you to think Procter
is fast. He is fast, but I don't want you to
think he is.

**Brian Bolus, Derbyshire captain, psyching his
batsmen up to face the fearsome Mike Procter**

The best way to lead your side is with 500 runs
behind you.

Graham Gooch, 1993

Why do so many players want to be captain?

Derek Underwood asks a reasonable question

I'm sleeping with him tonight.

**Faf du Plessis, South Africa's stand-in captain,
on how he'll reward a match-winning performance
by fast bowler Kagiso Rabada, 2016**

THE MEN
IN WHITE
COATS

The umpire is the law of cricket personified,
image of the noble constitution of the best
of games.

Neville Cardus, *Good Days*, 1934

Like politicians, their decisions rarely satisfy both parties.

Vic Marks, 1987

Cricket's my wife.

Dickie Bird

Great bloke, completely bonkers.

Ian Botham on Dickie Bird

As soon as I walked off the plane a spot of
rain hit me on the head. They had never seen rain
like it. People were on their hands and
knees shouting, 'Dickie Bird has arrived, it's
raining, it's raining!'

Dickie breaks the Bulawayo drought in 1992

The anguish on his countenance is something the
great actors would have given anything for.

John Arlott on Dickie Bird's face when faced with rain

You can see the moon. How far do you want
to see?

**Arthur Jepson refusing an appeal for bad light
during the famous Gillette Cup tie between Lancashire
and Gloucestershire, which finished at almost 9 o'clock
at night**

The modern umpire is caught between two opposing forces – the domestic pressures which encourage error and the technology which reveals them.

Imran Khan foreseeing a future with neutral umpires, *All Round View*, 1988

I would rather spend eight hours a day undergoing root-canal treatment than function as an international umpire.

Matthew Engel, *Wisden*, 2005

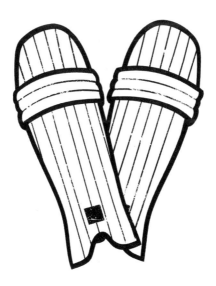

You'll never die wondering, son.

**Umpire Cec Pepper to Ashley Mallet, a frequent and
voluble appealer**

One friend said Cec was the only man
he knew who could talk, spit, chew, belch
and pass wind simultaneously.

**Obituary of legendary umpire
Cec Pepper, *Wisden*, 1994**

I'm sorry Mr Brearley. I knew it wasn't out.
But my hand started moving
upwards and I couldn't do anything
to stop it.

**An apologetic umpire to Mike Brearley
in a tour match in India**

For treatment.
He thinks the
last ball might
have broken
his finger.

**An umpire to John Price, who had asked why the
batsman had left the field, after he had been given not out
caught off the glove**

Umpire Frank Chester signals a leg-bye with the
Terpsichorean abandon of an Anton Dolin, and
chucks up the stone for the first ball of the over as if
he wished it were a cricket ball and he were about to
get amongst the first batsmen of summer 1914.

R C Robertson-Glasgow, *Crusoe on Cricket*, 1966

Chester was the most famous umpire of the century;
but for the loss of a hand in the First World War he
might have been one of its most famous players.

***Barclays World of Cricket*, 1986**

Michael, change of plan. Some Bodyline, son.

**Umpire Ian Gould informs Michael Clarke that Varun
Aaron is going to bowl around the wicket, 2014**

THE
BRUTAL
GAME

Use every weapon within the rules and stretch the
rules to breaking point, I say.

Fred Trueman, *Fast Fury,* **1961**

If there is any game in the world that attracts the
half-baked theorist more than cricket I have yet to
hear of it.

Fred Trueman, *Fred Trueman's Book*
of Cricket, **1964**

Cricket, more than any other sport, helps a person
work through the experience of loss by virtue of
forcing its participants to come to terms with
symbolic deaths on a daily basis.

Mike Brearley

24 June, 1915. Vermelles. This afternoon we had a cricket match, officers v sergeants, in an enclosure between some houses out of observation from the enemy. Our front-line is three-quarters of a mile away. I made top score, 24; the bat was a bit of a rafter, the ball a piece of rag tied with string; and the wicket a parrot cage with the clean, dry corpse of a parrot inside. Machine-gun fire broke up the match.

Robert Graves, on the Western Front, 1915

Cricket is a subtle game. In form and
appearance it can be gentle, even idyllic,
yet violence is always there.

Mihir Bose

We're still the lowest form of animal life!

**Len Hutton rouses the Players before their
annual match against the Gentlemen**

Baseball on Valium.

Robin Williams

Cricket is a game full of forlorn hopes and sudden dramatic changes of fortune and its rules are so ill-defined that their interpretation is partly an ethical business.

George Orwell

The Englishness is in the lie, in the cult of the honest yeoman, and the village green, in the denial of cricket's origins in commerce, politics, patronage and an urban society.

Mike Marqusee, *Anyone But England*, 1994

Few of those within the world of first-class cricket are political animals. That, however, is no excuse for being politically unconscious.

John Arlott on the D'Oliveira affair, 1968

Cricket more than any other game is inclined towards sentimentalism and cant.

Neville Cardus, 1981

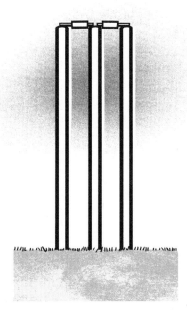

We don't play this game for fun.

Wilfred Rhodes

The game preys on doubt. It is a precarious game. Form, luck, confidence are transitory things. It's never easy to work out why they have so inexplicably deserted you.

Peter Roebuck, *It Never Rains*, 1984

Whisper it if you happen to be in the Lord's pavilion, but cricket is not a person. It is not a moral arbiter, a purveyor of ethics, a breeding ground for goodness … Cricket is a sport, and a bloody good one.

Lawrence Booth, *Cricket, Lovely Cricket?*, 2008

It is a cussed game. It can show you glimpses of
beauty in a stroke perfectly played, perhaps, and
then it throws you back into a trough of mediocrity.
Only the most phlegmatic or those who don't
give a damn or those with unshakeable belief
survive these upheavals easily.

Peter Roebuck, *It Never Rains*, 1984

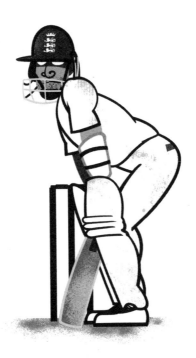

Cricket does not give itself away; it expects players to apply themselves, to think and study and seek. It plays tricks, too, pretends that sixes and slower balls and the other shortcuts matter. Cricket sets traps, flatters players and calls them kings when they are barely princes.

Peter Roebuck

Cricket makes no sense to me. I find it beautiful to watch and I like that they break for tea ... My friends from The Clash tried to explain it years and years ago, but I didn't understand what they were talking about.

American indie film director Jim Jarmusch

I understand cricket – what's going on, the scoring – but I can't understand why.

Bill Bryson

A missed catch, like a missed putt, can
leave a lifetime legacy of sudden shivers
in the night.

**R C Robertson-Glasgow, *The Observer on
Cricket*, 1987**

Jimmy Burke had an action like a policeman
applying a truncheon to a particularly short
offender's head.

Ian Peebles on Australian 'chucker' Jimmy Burke

I'm afraid this is the end, Dad.

Richie Benaud's consoling remarks to Ian 'Dad' Meckiff after he had been no-balled for throwing

Cricket is the easiest sport in the world to take over. Nobody bothered to pay the players what they were worth.

Kerry Packer

I've read a lot about Genghis Khan. He wasn't very lovable, but he was bloody efficient.

Kerry Packer, 1977

We should be celebrating his action, not trying to
run him out of the game.

**Bruce Yardley, Sri Lanka coach, on Muttiah Muralitharan
after he was called for throwing by Australian umpire
Darrell Hair, 1995**

It was an act of cowardice and I consider it
appropriate that Australian team were wearing yellow.

**New Zealand's PM Robert Muldoon passes verdict after
Trevor Chappell's underarm delivery denied the Kiwis
the chance to hit six off the last ball to win their one-day
international in 1981**

This small, silly error was blown out of all proportion
by the prying camera and by the hysterical clamouring
for a man who has carried our beloved, limping
cricket team through a blisteringly difficult year.

**Mark Nicholas' verdict on the dirt in pocket affair, where
England skipper Mike Atherton was caught drying his
hands with soil and accused of ball tampering**

As far as I was concerned, there were a few people
singing and dancing and that was it.

**Mike Gatting after demonstrations against his rebel team
in South Africa were broken up by police with dogs, tear
gas and batons**

Now I know
how Neil
Armstrong felt
when he stood
on the moon.

**Clive Rice, South Africa captain, on their return to Test
cricket in 1991**

When a tabloid cleared the decks of its usual diet of gossip, tits and football, you knew things must be bad.

Lawrence Booth on *The Sun*'s mock obituary for English cricket after plunging to the bottom of test rankings in 1999, *Cricket, Lovely Cricket?*, 2008

For people to whom cricket was a religion, we were heretics.

Greg Chappell on joining World Series Cricket

This is a Test match. It's not Old Reptonians versus Lymeswold, one off the mark and jolly good show.

David Gower on the challenges of facing the West Indies' fast bowling in 1984

Too much cricket will kill cricketers before they are ready to be killed.

Mike Gatting, 1987

We were going to sack him anyhow.

**Alec Bedser, chairman of selectors, after David Gower
resigned in 1989**

Cricket to me is a job, not a sport. Enjoyment rarely
comes into it.

Richard Hadlee

You can ask any fast bowler. If he says he has never
tampered with the ball, he either has just started
playing, or is lying.

Michael Holding on ball tampering

Every single bowler I know from the time I played,
between 1968 and 1984, was guilty of some sort of
ball changing.

Bob Woolmer

Quit squealing. These two could have bowled us out
with an orange.

**Geoff Boycott on allegations that Waqar Younis and
Wasim Akram's success in England in 1992 was down to
ball tampering**

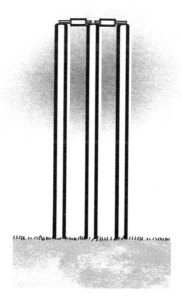

A career in cricket is in part about the accrual of
scar tissue, the thousand and one small cuts of
disappointment and defeat that weigh on the psyche
and extract their price.

Jon Hotten, *The Meaning of Cricket*, 2016

So many cricketers, their careers behind them,
have committed suicide. Bored by ordinariness,
unable to find a new refuge or simply despairing of
the future, they choose their moment and put an
end to it all.

Peter Roebuck, *Tangled Up in White*, 1990

Like few other sports of the field, cricket is played very much with the mind. Only the unimaginative player escapes the tensions. Many, whatever their seeming unconcern, retreat into caverns of introspection.

David Foot, *Harold Gimblett,* **1982**

In all the over lasted for seven minutes, 14 deliveries, and to Scott Boswell it has in a way never ended.

Jon Hotten, on Scott Boswell's 14-ball over in a one-day final, *The Meaning of Cricket,* **2016; two weeks later he was released by Leicestershire**

Controversy has always been part of cricket. It titillates and enlivens the human fabric. Much of it is unseemly but we are inclined to relish it in retrospect.

David Foot, *Cricket's Unholy Trinity,* **1985**

It's very simple really, Ed. Get runs in the
fifth Test and you'll be picked for two tours,
on which you've a good chance of doing
well. You could be established inside
six months. Fail and, given that you were
picked in good form, you might never
play again.

**David Fulton offers a blunt assessment to Kent
teammate Ed Smith before the last
Test against South Africa in 2003; Smith failed and
never played for England again, *On and Off
the Field*, 2003**

The Spirit of Cricket demands interpretation, which,
in turn, renders it worthless. One man's sledge is
another man's aside.

Mike Atherton, *The Times*, 2009

Beyond this, the greatest oddity of all is the fact that walking is no more than a theory, an idea, a suggestion. Broad waited to be given out, as all batsmen do. This was neither good nor bad sportsmanship – it was just playing professional cricket. There will be talk of brass neck, cheek, vast nicks, nicks so gigantic they scarcely register with conventional measuring instruments. But really there are incidents of this scale in pretty much every Test.

Barney Ronay on Stuart Broad's refusal to walk in the 2013 Ashes Test at Trent Bridge, *The Guardian*, 2013

Stuart Broad is a Shit Bloke.

T-shirts worn by some Australian supporters during the 2013/14 Ashes

Nothing yet devised by man is worse for a sick
hangover than a day's cricket in the summer sun.

Michael Parkinson

Cricket, like the upper classes and standards in general, is in permanent decline.

Alan Ross

We're coming to thump you here, man!

**Bishop Desmond Tutu shows his competitive side in the
TMS box during the South Africa v England 1994
Lord's Test**

It's a hard, fast, sharp game, where balls grind into knuckles and you dive and graze your skin. It's not this fleecy, lovely thing that everyone thinks it is. It's a wonderful game because it's evolved – like the language.

Stephen Fry, 2002

Admitting to being a Tory in Scotland is seen as weird, like cross-dressing or liking cricket.

Fraser Nelson, editor of *The Spectator*, 2013

SLEDGES
AND
SLIGHTS

That's just about the worst delivery I've ever seen in Test cricket.

**Jonathan Agnew on Steve Harmison's
infamous wide, which opened the 2006/07 Ashes series**

He couldn't bowl a hoop downhill.

Fred Trueman on Ian Botham, 1985

Quick? I could bowl quicker in me mac.

Fred Trueman on Darren Gough's pace (or lack thereof)

Intermittent idiosyncrasy must be ascribed to
Robert Peel, the Yorkshire bowler who could on
occasion drink himself into a condition more or
less indistinguishable from eccentricity … who was
eventually ushered out of the first-class game by
Lord Hawke, for a nameless misdemeanour often
said to have been his running in the wrong way and
bowling at the pavilion in the mistaken belief it was
a batsman.

Benny Green, *Barclays World of Cricket*, 1986

I haven't got a blue blazer and I don't have dandruff.

**David Hookes after being asked why he didn't become a
cricket administrator**

I hope he doesn't go on and make a hundred.

**Chris Scott of Durham, after dropping Brian Lara on 18;
he went to score 501 not out**

'No matter what sort of day you've had out there
today,' I'll tell them, 'I've had a worse one.
I promise.'

**The lesson that Scott, now head coach
of the Cambridge MCC Universities academy,
tells his charges**

There were times when Closey could make
Walter Mitty appear a modest
realist.

Ray East on Bryan Close, *A Funny Turn*, 1983

Leave our flies alone, Jardine. They're the only flamin' friends you've got here.

Aussie cricket fan to Douglas Jardine during the Bodyline series

If this letter reaches you, the Post Office thinks more of you than I do.

Quote from a letter sent to England captain Mike Denness after the 1974/75 Ashes thrashing in Australia

Tufnell! Can I borrow your brain? I'm building an idiot.

Australian crowd member to Phil Tufnell, 1994/95

Shane, I think I'm pregnant

Banner at Adelaide during the 2006/07 Ashes

Yes, I am Mrs Hoggard. And I've been listening to your crap for an hour. My husband's made you look a right tit.

Sarah Hoggard to Piers Morgan after hearing him badmouth husband Matthew during the 2005 Trent Bridge Ashes Test

Phil does it to me all the time but I, unfortunately, cannot go and whinge to Viv Richards.

**Frances Edmonds after Gordon Greenidge
had complained to her that her husband Phil had
been sledging him**

We all meet on the first morning, say 'How do you do' and nowt else for three days, except 'How's that.'

**Yorkshire opener Roy Kilner on the serious
business of a Roses match**

Mike Denness has as much claim to Illingworth's job as the vice captain of Stoke Poges' second eleven.

Michael Parkinson, 1972

'Do you want Gatt a foot wider?'
'No, he'd burst.'

Chris Cowdrey and David Gower on Mike Gatting, 1985

He's not that good. He tends to just start with a
four-letter word and then says a load
of nonsense.

**Mark Taylor on whether Shane Warne is one of the
best sledgers ever**

It's like a benefit match, is this. There'll be
someone going round with a raffle
before long.

**David Lloyd on the Test match between England and
Bangladesh at Chester-le-Street, 2005**

It's very sad when a good wine goes sour.

**Duncan Fletcher reacts to criticism of his England
team by Indian legend Sunil Gavaskar**

Even on the local nudist beach he only
admired himself.

Simon Hughes on Dermot Reeve

I regret that my mouth overtakes my brain.

Dermot Reeve, who was well known for letting his mouth overtake his brain

What number is Snow White batting?

John Emburey to a Middlesex teammate after seeing the diminutive Glamorgan batsmen Tony Cottey, Alastair Dalton and Stuart Phelps come and go

'Let's cut out some quick singles.'
'OK, Ken, we'll cut out yours.'

**Fred Titmus to Ken Barrington after a long, hot day
batting in Australia**

Was I bowled or run out?

**Doug Insole after being bowled by Tony Lock's
quicker ball, which he is considered by some to have
thrown, 1955**

A conversation with him would be 50 percent less if
you deleted the expletives.

Mike Selvey on John Emburey

'You know three-quarters of seven-eighths
of sod all,' he would habitually proclaim, his
hackles rising.
Sometimes he changed the fractions.
'You only said five-eighths last time,' I once observed
with pretence at pride.
'It still adds up to f****** nowt,' he blasted back.

**David Hopps recalls his favourite cricketer, former
Yorkshire 'keeper David Bairstow, 2015**

I know why he's bought a house by the sea … so
he'll be able to go for a walk on water.

**Fred Trueman after hearing that Geoff Boycott
had moved to Poole Harbour**

Off the field, he could be your lifelong buddy, but out in the middle, he had all the lovable qualities of a demented rhinoceros.

Colin McCool on his volatile Australian teammate, Bill O'Reilly

One of the few men you would back to get past a Lord's gateman with no more than an icy stare.

Martin Johnson on Peter Willey

All the never-say-die qualities of a kamikaze pilot.

An Australian journalist's withering assessment of England's cricketers in the 1990s

I don't know why he [Shane Warne] hates me ... Maybe it's because my face is real and his is not.

Marlon Samuels on his long-running feud with Warne

What a dipstick. To get a start like that and spoon it almost. That was like my mum hanging out the washing.

Geoff Boycott, invoking his mum in criticism of England's players

I reckon my mum could have caught that in her pinny.

As above, this time after seeing an easy catch go begging

It's like big girls before a hockey match.

Geoff Boycott is unimpressed with the England team's huddle before the start of play, 2008

He could have caught that between the cheeks of his backside.

Geoff Boycott

I'll have that bloody little wizard!

Geoff Boycott threatens *Harry Potter* star Daniel Radcliffe on *TMS* in 2009

We'll have a day where we all cancel Question Time
and come and watch the cricket.

**Former PM David Cameron under fierce questioning from
Geoff Boycott about why he hadn't agreed to visit Headingley**

He's still living off the fact that he coached a team
that anyone, even my dog Jerry, could have coached
to world domination.

Michael Clarke on his former coach John Buchanan, 2015

I saw him muttering something there that he
wouldn't have muttered in the stalls of St Paul's
when he was a choirboy.

**Jonathan Agnew surveying Alastair Cook's frustration in
the Champions Trophy**

MORE
LEGENDS
OF CRICKET

A cricketer of effect rather than the graces.

John Arlott on Ian Chappell, *An Eye for Cricket,* **1979**

If, as I think, history will find him to have been one of cricket's barbarians, that will be all the sadder because of his memorable excellence as a batsman.

Robin Marlar passes judgement on
Ian Chappell, *Barclays World of Cricket,*
1986

Playing against a team with Ian Chappell as captain turns a cricket match into gang warfare.

Mike Brearley

The old slope of grass that was The Hill at the Sydney Cricket Ground, since shamefully built on by barbarians with no souls, doubled as the unofficial Doug Walters Stand and it was there that the legend was given substance on sunburnt, beery days as the country boy strolled bow-legged to the crease like a gunslinger looking for trouble.

Kevin Mitchell on Doug Walters, 2000

Nobody's perfect. You know what happened to the last guy who was – they crucified him.

Geoff Boycott, 1979

The only thing I'm bloody frightened of
is getting out.

Geoff Boycott

We sometimes argue about the cricketer we would
choose to bat for one's life (consensus answer:
Don Bradman for your life, Geoff Boycott
for his own).

Matthew Engel, 1989

As I stood at the non-striker's end I felt a
wave of admiration for my partner; wiry,
slight, dedicated, a lonely man doing a lonely
job all these years.

Mike Brearley on Geoff Boycott

I hit more
sixes than
Bradman.

**Geoff Boycott in 2011, neglecting to point out Bradman hit
six sixes in 52 Tests, while he needed 108 to hit eight**

He built a fortress around himself, in life as at the
wicket.

**Christopher Martin-Jenkins on Geoff Boycott, *Cricket
Characters*, 1987**

If Geoffrey had played cricket the way he talked he
would have people queuing up to into the ground
instead of queuing up to leave.

Fred Trueman on Geoff Boycott

The programme implied that ... he made love like
he played cricket: slowly, methodically, but
with the real possibility that he might stay
in all day.

**Martin Kelner reviewing a documentary about Geoff
Boycott in *The Guardian*, 2003**

It was like batting against the World XI at one end
and Ilford Second XI at the other.

**Mike Gatting on facing New Zealand's Richard Hadlee in
his pomp**

Imagine being enclosed in a small, illuminated space
and being fed a barrage of searching questions by an
indefatigable examiner. Your responses are nervous
gibberish. It soon became clear that facing Hadlee
was a bit like this.

Simon Hughes, *A Lot of Hard Yakka*, 1997

I don't ask Kathy to face Michael Holding,
so there's no reason why I should be
changing nappies.

Ian Botham on marriage and parenting

Who writes
your scripts?

**Graham Gooch to Botham after he took a wicket
with his first ball in Test cricket after returning from
suspension in 1986**

He lifted the game from a state of conventional
excitement to one of unbelievable suspense and drama
and finally into the realms of romantic fiction.

Henry Blofeld on Ian Botham

He doesn't give a damn; he wants to ride a horse,
down a pint, roar around the land, waking up the
sleepers, show them things can be done.

Peter Roebuck on Ian Botham

If I'd done a quarter of things of which
I'm accused, I'd be pickled in alcohol.
I'd be a registered drug addict and would
have sired half the children in the world's
cricket-playing countries.

Ian Botham

Gower never moves, he drifts.

Peter Roebuck on David Gower, *Ashes to Ashes*, 1987

Difficult to be more laid back without being actually comatose.

Frances Edmonds on Gower,
***Daily Express*, 1985**

A curly-haired kitten.

Frank Keating on David Gower

Hey Greigy! This champagne's all right, but the
blackcurrant jam tastes of fish.

**Derek Randall tasting caviar on his first tour to India
1976/77**

Randall bats like an octopus with piles.

**A South Australian cricket fan, as told to
Matthew Engel**

When he strolls away to square leg, it is like an act of thanksgiving that the previous ball has been survived and a moment of prayer for the fibre to get through the next.

Bob Willis on legendary plodder Chris Tavaré

As an ersatz opening batsman, Tavaré did not so much score runs as smuggle them out by stealth.

Gideon Haigh

Geoffrey Boycott is fond of expressing the conviction that if you stay there long enough, runs will automatically come. Not with Tavaré, they didn't. If he stayed there long enough, then at the end of it, he was still there. He was the ultimate existential cricketer.

Marcus Berkmann, *Rain Men*, 1995

It couldn't have been Gatt. Anything he takes up to his room after 9 o'clock he eats.

Ian Botham's verdict and the affair which cost Gatting the England captaincy

If it had been a cheese roll, it would never have got past him.

Graham Gooch on Shane Warne's wonder ball to Mike Gatting in 1993

You can see by his walk to the wicket, like a terrier
out for a walk in the neighbourhood bristling with
bigger dogs, that he is ready for a fight and not afraid
of his ability to look after himself.

Christopher Martin-Jenkins on Alan Border, *Cricket*
Characters, **1987**

Border is a walnut: hard to crack and without much to please the eye.

Peter Roebuck

Perhaps it is best to say that, if all living things in India are incarnations, [Sunil] Gavaskar is technical orthodoxy made flesh.

Scyld Berry, 1983

[Viv Richards] bats with the passionate intensity of a murderer rather than the cool rationality of an assassin.

Peter Roebuck on Viv Richards, *Slices of Cricket*, 1982

His game embraced a contempt for his fate, a foaming fury, because to him, cricket was a game of kill or be killed, a street fight in which it was left to the umpires to keep peace.

Peter Roebuck on Viv Richards

He bowls like a god but talks like a civil servant.

Michael Davie on Derek Underwood, *The Observer Book of Cricket*, 1987

The police trying to protect the uncrowned
King of Antigua at the end of what
has been an absolutely brilliant
hundred.

Christopher Martin-Jenkins on Viv Richards'
56-ball 100 against England in Antigua
in 1986

But sadly, everything came to a temporary halt when his knees buckled under the strain of his bowling. In a sense this was appropriate, since he had made so many female cricket followers go weak at the knees.

Matthew Engel surveys the many talents of Imran Khan, *Barclays World of Cricket*, **1986**

He is built like a guardsman and that expressionless face with the black moustache surely saw service in England's imperial wars, defending Rorke's Drift and marching up the Khyber Pass.

Geoffrey Moorhouse on Graham Gooch

Like some immutable law of physics, [Steve] Waugh has always saved his best for the most unpromising situations.

Derek Pringle

Concentration is sometimes mistaken for grumpiness.

Mike Atherton

ENGLAND,
THEIR
ENGLAND

England's always expecting. No wonder they call her the mother country.

Fred Trueman before his final Test

The last positive thing England did for cricket was invent it.

Ian Chappell

Whenever I see Ken coming to the wicket, I imagine the Union Jack fluttering behind him.

Wally Grout on Ken Barrington

My God, look what they've sent me.

A C MacLaren surveying the team he was given to try to win the 1902 Ashes at Old Trafford

We've always set the trend. Remember, women cricketers were the first to bowl overarm.

Rachael Heyhoe Flint, 1975

Ladies playing cricket? Absurd. Just like a man trying to knit.

Len Hutton

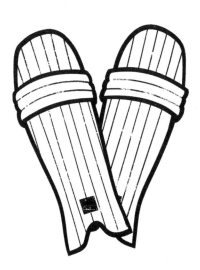

Lord Hawke, had he been asked about it, might have taken the same view as I do about having families on tour. It is no more the place for them than a trench on the Somme.

John Woodcock, *The Times*, 1975

I have played my best cricket when I have been with my wife.

Alan Knott, 1977

The authorities should consider that a cricketer is more likely to have a proper night's sleep with his wife in bed beside him, rather than a temporary stand-in and all the parallel gymnastics that would follow.

Lindsay Lamb, wife of England batsman Allan, makes the case for wives accompanying players on tour

'There's a woman in the committee room!'

'Jim, it's Saturday, it's a Lord's Test, it's the Queen.'

'Nevertheless!'

An encounter between E W Swanton and a Marylebone Cricket Club member, as recounted by Stephen Fry

Girls! It's absolutely outrageous.

Robin Marlar on women's cricket

Absurd, old fashioned and patronising.

Clare Connor on Robin Marlar

There are men who fear women more than
they love cricket.

D L A Jephson

We have nothing against man cricketers. Some
of them are quite nice people, even though
they don't win as often as we do.

**Rachael Heyhoe Flint, throwing shade at a
failing England team**

No longer should we allow international cricketers
to appear on our television sets to be interviewed
unshaven, chewing gum and altogether looking
slovenly. These habits are to be deplored and should
be eliminated.

**Ian MacLaurin, after his appointment as English Cricket
Board Chairman, 1988**

He will see that trying to shake up English cricket is
like stirring dead sheep.

**Ray Illingworth on Ian MacLaurin's attempts to rouse
English cricket**

He may be good enough for England, but not for
Yorkshire.

**Brian Sellers on the decision to get rid of Johnny Wardle, even
though he had been selected for England four days before**

The situation is a smaller version of the
United States and Russia. They have
their differences, but they still have to
live on the same planet.

Yorkshire CCC chairman Michael Crawford
on the county's long-running cricket civil war,
1982

Don't tell me his average or top score at
Trent Bridge. How many runs, how many
wickets did he get against Yorkshire?

Douglas Jardine's yardstick for
judging cricketers

I would have died for Yorkshire. I suppose once or twice I nearly did.

Brian Close

In an England cricket eleven, the flesh may be of the south, but the bone is of the north, and the backbone is Yorkshire.

Len Hutton

The trouble with you damn Yorkshiremen is
that you are only interested in playing this
game to win.

**An unnamed, former England captain to
Fred Trueman, reportedly**

Civil war is
never far below
the surface
of Yorkshire
cricket.

Cricket Society **editor James P Coldham**

We are a cricket club, not a debating society.

**David Bairstow, Yorkshire captain, at the time of the
county club's civil war, 1985**

It can be absurd, cantankerous, self-destructive and
pompous, but it is never crass.

Peter Roebuck on Yorkshire cricket

As preparation for a Test match, the domestic
game is the equivalent of training for an Olympic
marathon by taking the dog for a walk.

Martin Johnson, *The Independent*, 1995

Bloody Derby! What a way to go!

**Jonathan Agnew before his last match against
Derbyshire, 1990**

More reported cases of frostbite than any other first-class venue.

Jonathan Agnew on the delights of Derby

The whole of our national sport is not doing very well. We may be in the wrong sign or something. Venus may be in the wrong juxtaposition to somewhere else.

England supremo Ted Dexter's unique take after England's seventh successive Test defeat in 1993

They go over there and all that happens is they face bowlers who are really 'pie throwers'.

Rod Marsh on the challenges, or lack thereof, facing Aussie batsmen who ventured to England to play county cricket, 1993

Most county cricketers play the game for the life rather than the living. For them it's the motorways of England rather than the jet lanes of the world. It's sausage, egg and chips at Watford Gap rather than vol-au-vents and small talk on the Governor-General's lawn in Barbados.

Michael Carey

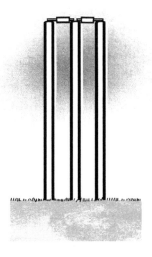

The vast majority of county cricketers have two topics of conversation: 'Me and My Cricket,' or, as a high day and holiday variant, 'My Cricket and Me.'

Frances Edmonds, 1994

One is always a little nervous when watching England bat.

Peter May, 1984

Who can forget Malcolm Devon?

Ted Dexter on Devon Malcolm

A fart competing with thunder.

**Graham Gooch's blunt appraisal of his side's
performance in the 1990/91 Ashes**

If I were being polite, I'd say that Gatt is a
little long in the tooth, somewhat immobile
and carries too much weight. But I prefer
straight-talking, so I'm saying what
I really think. Gatt is too old, too slow,
and too fat.

**Geoff Boycott passes judgement on Gatting's selection for
the 1994/95 Ashes**

It's nice to go into the rest day as favourites. I might
get some sleep.

**England coach Keith Fletcher during the 1994 Trinidad
Test against the West Indies; they were bowled out for
46 to lose the match**

If England ever do rise to the occasion out there,
we can be pretty sure someone will crick his
back on the way up.

Giles Smith on England's injury-ravaged 1996 World Cup

At the 1996 World Cup, the England squad
resembled a bad-tempered grandmother
attending a teenage rave.

Matthew Engel, *Wisden,* **1997**

Cricket [in England] is widely viewed as elitist, exclusionist and dull.

Matthew Engel, *Wisden,* **1997**

When the pressure point comes, English cricketers crumble.

Shane Warne, 1997

Too much crap cricket on crap wickets.

Tom Moody's take on England's woes in 1997

There is no limit to what England's cricketers can achieve, as long you keep them off the pitch.

Giles Smith, *The Times*

All you want is someone out there in top hat and tails and a big whip and get the elephants moving and we're in business.

Fred Trueman on another England batting collapse

Barring injuries or sexual indiscretions between now and next Thursday, the three other newcomers [Barnett, Russell and Lawrence] seem certain to get the benefit of Peter May's Emporium Giant 1988 England Cap Sale.

Matthew Engel on English's cricket summer horribilis, 1988

At least we are safe from an intoxicating rendition of 'There's only one Graeme Hick'. There are, quite clearly, two of them. The first one turns out for teams like Worcestershire and New Zealand's Northern Districts and plays like a god. The second one pulls on an England cap and plays like an anagram of god.

Martin Johnson

One began to feel that the right adjective was the one never attached to him in his playing days: amateurish.

Matthew Engel on Ray Illingworth's reign as supremo of English cricket

Those who run cricket in this country, especially at the domestic level, are for the most part a self-serving, pusillanimous and self-important bunch of myopic dinosaurs unable to take anything but the shortest-term view of everything.

Henry Blofeld, 2003

It's typical of English cricket. A tree gets in the way for 200 years and when it falls down, instead of cheering, they plant a new one.

Australian coach Dave Gilbert is baffled by the saga of the Canterbury tree

Defeat by Pakistan would surely set a new level of ignominy that may not be beaten until the Afghans, or Eskimos, visit Lord's.

Simon Wilde may not be quite off the mark in his prediction of what England's loss to Pakistan at the World Twenty20 2009 could do

It wasn't quite the butcher, baker and candlestick-maker, but it was the repo man, the restaurateur and the insurance broker who embarrassed England in an astonishing start to the World Twenty20.

Mike Atherton uses a nursery rhyme reference to describe the semi-pro Dutchmen's victory against England, 2009

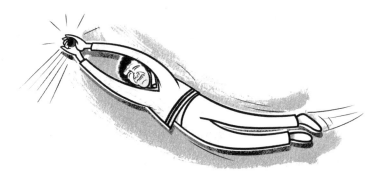

Following England in this World Cup is like following Newcastle United – you never know what you're going to get. One minute we're beating South Africa, the next we're losing to Bangladesh and Ireland.

Graeme Swann on England's wildly inconsistent 2011 World Cup campaign

We're happy to tootle along in a two-litre diesel in a Formula 1 race.

Graeme Swann on England's one-day strategy in 2014

I am amused to see Colin Graves described as a 'no-nonsense Yorkshireman'. Ever since he was appointed it's been nothing but nonsense.

**Henry Blofeld on incoming ECB chairman
Colin Graves, 2015**

An optimist, they say, describes the glass as half-full. A pessimist describes it as half-empty. And a regular supporter of England at cricket World Cups expects the glass to fragment, explode and kill everyone in the near vicinity.

George Dobell, *28 Days' Data*, 2016

THE
ASHES

In affectionate remembrance of ENGLISH
CRICKET which died at The Oval on
29th August, 1882.
Deeply lamented by a large circle of sorrowing
Friends and Acquaintances R.I.P
N.B – The body will be cremated, and the Ashes
taken to Australia.

The Times, **1882**

They are capital winners out here, but I'm afraid I
cannot apply the same adjective to them as losers.

Lord Harris on Australians

Test cricket is not a light-hearted business, especially
that between England and Australia.

Don Bradman, *Farewell to Cricket*, 1950

The aim of English Test cricket is, in fact, mainly to beat Australia.

Jim Laker, *Over to Me,* 1960

Almost from the start Australia's approach reflected the heat and dust of the interior, the baked ground and vast open spaces that encouraged boldness even as England's drizzle, mud and enclosed fields preached caution.

Peter Roebuck, *In It to Win It,* 2006

Which one of you bastards called this bastard a bastard?

Bill Woodfull to the crowd, after a comment made to England skipper Douglas Jardine, during the Bodyline series of 1932/33

All Australians are an uneducated and unruly mob.

Douglas Jardine, which might explain the comment above

In our opinion [bodyline bowling] is
unsportsmanlike. Unless it is stopped at once, it is
likely to upset the friendly relationships existing
between Australia and England.

Cable from the ACB to the MCC after the 1933 Adelaide Test

Well, we shall win the Ashes – but we may lose a
Dominion.

**Rockley Wilson after hearing that Douglas Jardine was to
captain the MCC team to Australia in 1932/33**

There are two teams out there; one is trying to play
cricket and the other is not.

**Australian captain Bill Woodfull to Pelham Warner
during the Adelaide Test, 1932/33**

To take the most charitable view of the
position, the behaviour of Australian crowds
at its best, when judged by the standards
accepted in the rest of the world, is not
naturally good.

**Douglas Jardine after his return from
the 1932/33 Ashes**

I see His Highness is a conscientious objector.

**Douglas Jardine to the Nawab of Pataudi, who refused to
field in the leg trap in the Sydney Bodyline Test**

The term is meaningless. What is bodyline?

Jardine again

Leg-theory, even as bowled by Larwood, came as a
natural evolution in the game. There was nothing
sinister about it and nothing sinister was intended.

Bill Bowes, 1949

A cricket tour in Australia would be the most
delightful period in your life – if you were deaf.

Harold Larwood, 1933

Bailey, I wish you were a statue and I was a pigeon.

Sydney crowd member to Trevor Bailey, 1954/55

I have on occasions taken quite a reasonable dislike to the Australians.

Ted Dexter, 1972

There's no batsman on earth who goes out to face
Dennis Lillee and Jeff Thomson with a smile
on his face.

Clive Lloyd

I don't think we have met – my name's
Cowdrey.

**Colin Cowdrey, summoned to help England aged 41,
introduces himself to Jeff Thomson after reaching the
crease in the 1974/75 Ashes**

Lillee and Thomson remain a combination
to conjure with, as sinister in England as
Burke and Hare, or Bismarck
and Tirpitz.

Gideon Haigh

Ashes to Ashes, dust to dust, if Thomson don't get ya, Lillee must.

A Sydney *Daily Telegraph* cartoon caption during the 1974/75 Ashes

Who's this then? Father Bloody Christmas?

Jeff Thomson on seeing David Steele at the crease in 1975

Blimey, who have we got here, Groucho Marx?

A reported alternative to the above

Stuff that stiff upper lip crap. Let's see how stiff it is when it's split.

Jeff Thomson

It was the summer of summers for England.

Richie Benaud on Botham's Ashes, 1981

Come on, let's give it some humpty.

Ian Botham to Graham Dilley, Headingley, 1981

If I played and missed he was standing at the other end, grinning. If I tried a really big heave and made no contact he would just lean on his bat and laugh out loud.

Graham Dilley remembers his and Botham's match-turning partnership at Headingley, 1981

It's gone straight into the confectionery stand and out again.

Richie Benaud on one of Botham's massive hits

I looked into his eyes and it was like there was no one there.

Graham Dilley remembers Bob Willis during his matchwinning 8–43 at Headingley, 1981

It will be remembered in 100 years – unfortunately.

Kim Hughes, on the 1981 Ashes series

I suppose me mum'll speak to me. Reckon me dad will too. And my wife. But who else?

Kim Hughes after the Headingley defeat, 1981

Botham's Ashes: the images and the yarns are as well-worn as the pages of a boy's first mucky book: the blind fury of those hook shots that nearly launched him off his feet, that square cut through point off Lillee, the irresistible force of his bowling action, enormously strong but still lithe. It is all as vivid as any childhood memory.

Alan Tyers recalls the 1981 Ashes, 2009

There are few remaining English prophets in Australia forecasting anything but doom, but for heaven's sake let's not panic. England have only three major problems. They can't bat, they can't bowl and they can't field.

Martin Johnson before the 1986/87 Ashes series – which England won

That's it, boys. I'm off. The taxi's waiting.

An under-pressure David Gower leaves a press conference during the dismal second Ashes Test, 1989

The current definition of an optimist in Australia is
an Englishman who puts on sunscreen before
going out to bat.

Martin Johnson

David, the last time I came here, I was the nice guy
who finished last.

**Alan Border explains to David Gower why his Aussie team
had become so uncompromising, 1989**

Gooch has had so many opening partners since
1979 that he must have felt at times like the Wing
Commander of a World War I Tiger Moth
Squadron ... A rueful greeting in the knowledge of
minimal life-expectancy and the inevitable letter ('Dear
Mrs Morris/Stephenson/Larkins ...') to the next of kin.

Martin Johnson

Gower was out, last ball before lunch, to a trap that
could not have been more obvious had his leg-side
fielders been linked together in a circle holding
fireman's blanket.

Martin Johnson

Man for man, on paper, the Australia side stand out like dog's balls.

Greg Chappell delivers his forecast for the 1994 Ashes

He was all bristle and bullshit and I couldn't make
out what he was saying, except that every sledge
ended with 'arsewipe'.

Mike Atherton on Merv Hughes

His sledging was always more subtle and intelligent
than my basic stuff. It would often take me three
overs to understand what he meant.

Merv Hughes on Mike Atherton

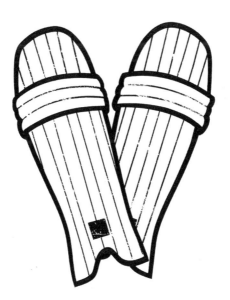

I'll have a few drinks in a very short space of time.

**Jason Gillespie on how he would celebrate his match-winning
performance at Headingley in the 1997 Ashes**

They'd win the first four Tests and we'd try to nick
one at the end when they were all drunk.

**Nasser Hussain looking back at some difficult
Ashes series, 2013**

One day we'll lose the Ashes and it will be as horrific
as waking up after a night on the drink in a room
full of images of Camilla Parker Bowles.

Sydney Morning Herald **on the eve of the 2005 Ashes**

This Test series has an epic grandeur capable of making
all other big sporting events puny by comparison.

Michael Parkinson on the momentous 2005 Ashes series

All the palaver caused me to burn my toast.

England coach Duncan Fletcher reflects on the ruckus caused when sub Gary Pratt ran out Ricky Ponting at Trent Bridge during the 2005 Ashes

An innings of neurotic violence, of eccentric watchfulness, of brainless impetuosity and incontinent savagery.

Simon Barnes on Kevin Pietersen's century at the Oval in the fifth Test in 2005, which clinched the Ashes for England

I was a bit worried that it would be embarrassing and that there would be only three men and a dog out on the streets to see us.

Matthew Hoggard on the procession through London to celebrate winning the 2005 Ashes; thousands turned up

Warney dropped the Ashes.

England crowd at the Oval in the final Test in 2005, after
Shane Wame dropped Kevin Pietersen who went on to
secure an Ashes-winning draw

We wish you were English.

The same crowd try to make it up to Warne, who took 41
wickets in the series

Is it cowardly to pray for rain?

Commenter to *The Guardian*'s cricket website, reflecting
the shattered nerves of thousands of England cricket fans
during that summer of 2005

Nice place, Buckingham Palace. The Queen has
clearly done very well for herself.

**Matthew Hoggard, after the 2005 Ashes winning team's
visit to meet the Queen**

The most exciting thing about it is that I'll be
awarded the freedom of Preston. That means I can
drive a flock of sheep through the town centre, drink
for free in no less than 64 pubs, and get a lift home
from the police when I'm drunk. What more could
you want?

**Andrew Flintoff on the fame and fortune that came with
winning the 2005 Ashes**

Australia all out for 348 on a golden evening at the Oval.

Christopher Martin-Jenkins on the moment of England's 2009 Ashes win

How can you have a clash of cultures when you're playing against a country with no culture?

Former England captain David Gower ill-advisedly ups the ante before the 2013 Ashes

We finished third in a two-horse race.

Matt Prior offers a blunt assessment of England's 2013/14 Ashes campaign

He's only just turned up, let's not give him too much credit.

Alastair Cook jokes about the positive effects of new coach Trevor Bayliss after winning the 2015 Ashes

THE
GLOBAL
GAME

Done the elephants. Done the poverty. Might as well go home.

Phil Tufnell jokes about the experience of touring India

Is it worth seeing, then?

**Unnamed England player to Mike Atherton after he had
visited the Taj Mahal, one of the Seven Wonders of the World**

I am happy they [England] gave us [India] the game of cricket, which they can't play very well, and the English language, which I can't speak very well.

Former India captain Kapil Dev, 2014

The Australian temper is at bottom grim. It is as though the sun has dried up his nature.

Neville Cardus

There can be no doubt of the central significance of cricket in creating an Australian identity.

Derek Birley, *The Willow Wand*, 1979

The only time an Australian walks is when his car runs out of petrol.

Barry Richards, 1980

The traditional dress of the Australian cricketer is the Baggy Green cap on the head and the chip on the shoulder.

Simon Barnes

If the West Indies are on top, they're
magnificent. If they are down, they grovel.
And with the help of Brian Close
and a few others, I intend to make
them grovel.

**Tony Greig before the 1976 series, which
England lost 3–0**

We have a saying in the West Indies – if you want to
drive, buy a car.

**Michael Holding on his and his teammates' penchant
for the short ball**

Cricket was – and remains – the only expression of
unity in the West Indies.

Gerald Howat, *Cricket's Second Golden Age*, 1989

It's Test cricket; it's tough. If you want an easy game,
take up netball.

**Steve Waugh on his side's hard-fought win in the
Caribbean, 1995**

I remember some good Saturdays against the West
Indies before – the only trouble is that the Thursdays,
Fridays, Mondays and Tuesdays were a bit of a disaster.

John Emburey, 1984

I have never upset anyone in my life.

Javed Miandad, who upset nearly everyone

Pakistan is the sort of place every man should send his mother-in-law to, for a month, all expenses paid.

Ian Botham, 1984

Why don't you send in your mother-in-law now? She couldn't do any worse.

Pakistani player to Botham after he was dismissed for a duck in the 1992 World Cup final

I was calling him potato in Punjabi because he is a little fat.

A spectator after an aggrieved Inzamam-ul-Haq waded into the crowd waving a bat

I remember the 1992 World Cup final. It's my earliest memory. Inzamam-ul-Haq was skinny. Well, skinny-ish.

England spinner Moeen Ali looks back, 2014

We murdered 'em. We got on top and
steamrollered 'em. We have flippin' hammered
'em. One more ball and we'd have walked it.
We murdered 'em and they know it. We flippin'
hammered 'em.

**England coach David Lloyd after England fell a run short
of beating Zimbabwe in Bulawayo, 1996**

Now I think we should all go off to hospital to have
our pulses checked.

Henry Blofeld after the same game

The history of Pakistani cricket is one of
nepotism, inefficiency, corruption and constant
bickering.

Imran Khan

I want my team to play today like a cornered tiger.

**Imran Khan ahead of the 1992 World Cup final;
they did**

Most Pakistan sides have one unifying factor – they all hate the captain.

Simon Barnes, *The Times*, 2001

England is not ruined because sinewy brown men from a distant colony sometimes hit a ball further and oftener than we do.

J B Priestley

Being the manager of a touring team is rather like being in a charge of a cemetery – lots of people underneath you, but no one listening.

Wes Hall, manager of several West Indies cricket tours

Matthew Hayden copped some flak this week when a commentator questioned why the devout Christian crossed himself only after scoring a century for Australia and not for Queensland. That's easily explained – no one watches state cricket, not even God.

Doug Conway, *Canberra Times*

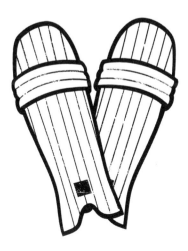

Australia were murdered, just as we were
murdered, Test in, Test out, all last summer. It
was like finding an old mate in the next bed in
intensive care.

**Ian Wooldridge, after Australia's
annihilation by the West Indies,
The Daily Mail, 1984**

We have decided that we will each wear a black
armband for the duration of the World Cup.
In doing so we are mourning the death of
democracy in our beloved Zimbabwe.
In doing so we are making a silent plea to
those responsible to stop the abuse of human
rights in Zimbabwe. In doing so we pray
that our small action may help to restore sanity
and dignity to our nation.

**Andy Flower and Henry Olonga,
2003 World Cup**

Didn't think much of it. Couldn't live there,
could you?

**Colin Dredge, Somerset's 'Demon of Frome', on the
Acropolis**

It was not unlike watching Lazarus rise from the
dead and get mown down by a runaway truck on his
way to the bar.

**Ian Wooldridge on New Zealand's performance
against Pakistan in the 1992
World Cup, *Daily Mail***

You're regarded as a soft guy in Holland if you play
cricket. They think it's all eating lunch and tea, and
pretty boring.

Dutch fast bowler Andre van Troost, 1993

This was royalty on the toilet, pants around their ankles.

Mike Selvey on Bangladesh's shock defeat of Australia in an ODI, 2005

THE
HALLOWED
TURF

The day was warm and the wicket still so beautiful that bowlers might well have watered it with tears.

Neville Cardus, *Good Days*, 1934

The wicket is still being blamed. It has been libelled, slandered and blasphemed, accused in turn of being a fickle and vicious Jezebel and a slumbering, lifeless dog.

David Foot, *Cricket's Unholy Trinity*, 1985

The stumps were a survival from a distant epoch in the game's development; they were like a little toe on the human foot.

Neville Cardus writing about the 1938 Oval Test, on the second day, when only four wickets had fallen, none bowled

I asked Jim Laker whether he felt we should bat or insert our opponents. He went out to have a look and was missing for a very long time. I asked Jim where he had been and he said that he had been looking for the pitch and was still not sure whether he had found it.

Trevor Bailey, *Wickets, Catches and the Odd Run*, 1986

What England will be like 100 years hence we cannot pretend to prophesy, but this we can say – that Lord's and the MCC will continue to flourish and increase their popularity.

Lord Harris, 1914

If I close my eyes I can see Lord's as it was then, and I know that when the memories of bed and battle have lost their colours and faded to misty grey, that at least will be as bright as ever.

George MacDonald Fraser, *Flashman's Lady*, 1977

It caught my youthful imagination,
and from that day I have loved every
stick and stone of Lord's, and as the year's
pass I love it more and more. Even now,
after so many years, I feel something of a thrill
as I walk down St John's Wood Road, and
my heart, maybe, beats a shade faster as I enter
the ground.

Pelham Warner

I feel as though I am stepping into history.

J M Kilburn on Lord's, *Overthrows,* **1975**

Lord's is the Valhalla of cricketers; countless days, famous for great deeds, have come to a resting place at Lord's.

Neville Cardus, *The Summer Game,* **1929**

At The Oval, men seemed to have rushed away with some zest from their city offices. At Lord's there is a dilettante look, as if men whose work, if any, has yet to come.

Revd James Pycroft, *Oxford Memories,* **1886**

Lord's – it's a magical world to me, the 'open sesame'
to a lifetime of happiness.

Margaret Hughes, *All on a Summer's Day*, 1953

Essentially, The Oval is truer London than is Lord's.
The Oval, as it were, is Dickens; Lord's is Thackeray

R C Robertson-Glasgow

Go To Lord's and analyse the crowd. There are all
sorts and conditions of men there round the ropes
– bricklayers, bank clerks, soldiers, postmen, and
stockbrokers. And in the pavilion are Q.C's, artists,
archdeacons, and leader-writers. Bad men, good men,
workers and idlers, are all there, and all at one in
their keenness over the game.

Prince Ranjitsinhju, ***The Jubilee Book of Cricket,*** **1897**

VIEWS
FROM THE
BOUNDARY

And a Freaker! We've got a freaker down the wicket now. Not very shapely. And it's masculine. And I would think it's seen the last of its cricket for the day ...

John Arlott describes the first ever Test match streaker, 1975

The England total 707 for 5, and the gasometer sinking lower and lower.

Howard Marshall, 1937

To be a commentator, you must have a life outside cricket, too. If cricket is all that you know, then you would not be a great commentator.

Harsha Bhogle

Exact, enthusiastic, prejudiced, amazingly visual, authoritative and friendly ... he sounds like Uncle Tom Cobleigh reading Neville Cardus to the Indians.

Dylan Thomas on John Arlott

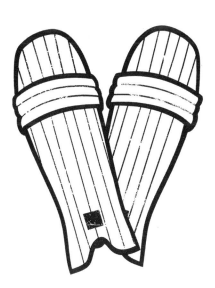

Probably the most celebrated British voice after Churchill's.

Frank Keating on John Arlott, 1991

He absorbed and distilled everything. He was in no sense verbose. The words were always spare and rationed. But they created the sense of a game and a ground and a cast and a drama unfolding with such deft accuracy that cricket itself somehow grew in significance.

The Guardian **editorial after John Arlott's death in 1991**

My word, I know what the problems are. I've failed
at everything.

**John Arlott on whether his lack of playing experience
counted against him as a commentator**

A man with
a music hall
imagination.

John Arlott on Brian Johnston

He was the last great voice of radio commentary.

David Lloyd on Brian Johnston

The crowd, like dolphins breaking surface,
was soon getting to its feet, struggling into
macintoshes and balancing paper hats.
Within twenty minutes the players were off: and
again there was the vilely familiar
spectacle of covers being pushed on,
the sky behind the Vauxhall cranes like
a damp dishcloth and the atmosphere
one of boredom, hope and endurance as
inextricably linked as the colours of the
national flag.

Alan Ross, 1956, as quoted in *Cricket,*
***Lovely Cricket!*, Lawrence Booth,**
2008

Today's editors would be in touch straight away if
anyone dared to file such luxuries. But it sure beats
'rain stopped play.'

Lawrence Booth on the above quote, ibid

I said my prayers regularly and I remember after 'Gentle Jesus ...' and 'God Bless ...' I always added 'Please God let me play cricket for Sussex regularly.' I added the 'regularly' because I thought the Almighty might fob me off with an odd game against Oxford and Cambridge.

Geoffrey Cox, *The Cricketer*, 1981

Four separate stoppages for rain and bad light left the day as shapeless as a Demis Roussos costume.

Glenn Moore, *The Independent*, 1994

[I am] not a good watcher of the game. I think cricket is a boring game to watch.

Former Indian great Sunil Gavaskar, now a sought-after cricket commentator

Trusting county committee men to do what is best for the national game is like putting Brer Fox in charge of chickens.

Scyld Berry

Dear Sir, on Friday I watched J M Brearley very carefully as he directed his fieldsmen. He then looked up at the sun and made a gesture which seemed to indicate that it should move a little squarer. Who is this man? Yours sincerely, S A Nicholas, Longlevens, Glos.

Letter to *The Guardian*, 1981

Simon Hughes thanks everyone who donated to today's benefit collection, which raised 1230 pounds, 30 pence, 70 Canadian cents, 50 pesetas, 1 Kenyan shilling and 2 Iranian shekels.

Tannoy announcer at Lord's during Hughes' benefit in 1991

If I had my time over again, I would never have played cricket. Why? Because of people like you. The press do nothing but criticise.

Garry Sobers

I will never be accepted by the snob press.

Ray Illingworth

You have to try and reply to criticism with your intellect, not your ego.

Mike Brearley with some sage advice on handling the media

I knew I could never be a 'real'
newspaper journalist – it was such a
difficult job to be hail-fellow-well-met-what's-yours
in private life and the next day have to
scalpel-slash a reputation in
public print.

Frank Keating, *Another Bloody Day
in Paradise,* **1981**

Another day, another dolour.

**Matthew Engel on tour with England in the
West Indies, 1986/87**

And the whole crowd seething with West Indian
delight. I can only say it was worth this; it was
worth the treatment it's getting. I thought I saw a
policeman applauding.

**John Arlott on Clive Lloyd's World Cup final
century in 1975**

The other hazard at the moment is a colony of silver
gulls, several hundreds of them. At first they pitched
on top of the stand as if they were vultures recruited
for Lillee ...

John Arlott, 1977

I can see a butterfly walking across the pitch, and what's more it appears to have a limp.

Henry Blofeld

I love these claret-coloured buses. They give me all sorts of ideas …

Henry Blofeld

From the broadcasting box, you can't see any grass at all – just a carpet of humanity.

Bernard Kerr describes the joyous moment England regained the Ashes in 1953

There are people holding their hearts when he plays a shot. The one he hit in the air over there, there were two chaps by the side of me who nearly passed out.

Fred Trueman on the tension as Geoff Boycott closed in on his 100th first-class 100 at Leeds in 1977

Test Match Special is all chocolate cake and jolly japes, but I didn't enjoy being called a wheelie bin and nor did my family.

Ashley Giles takes issue with Henry Blofeld's colourful descriptions

In many ways Richie has been the Hemingway of the airwaves, treating us to an economy of words and style …

Mike Atherton on Richie Benaud, 2005

There was a slight interruption there for athletics.

Richie Benaud's description of a streaker

I'm called that [Spiro] by two people. Ian Botham and Ian Chappell, both of whom hate each other. It's the one thing they have in common.

Jonathan Agnew on his other nickname, 2012

Fielders scattering like missionaries to far places.

John Arlott

I didn't even wear a box in those days – I wasn't all that well developed.

Michael Bentine recalls his days as a schoolboy cricketer, 1983

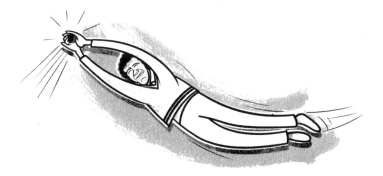

If you wanted to put it in a book, no one would ever believe it. It belongs to a novel, not *Wisden*.

John Arlott on England's dramatic two-wicket win over South Africa in 1948

A banal bunch of louts.

Ian Wooldrige works himself into apoplexy about the Barmy Army

Swann, Swann will tear you apart again.

Barmy Army sing (to the tune of Joy Division's 'Love Will Tear Us Apart Again')

IN MY
DAY

I'd have looked faster in colour.

**Fred Trueman after being told that his bowling didn't look
so quick in old footage**

There is nothing I have detested more than the way
in which elder men have said that their young days
had the best. Cricket is constantly in flux.

Home Gordon, *Background of Cricket*, 1939

Cricket reform has always attracted the attention of the eccentric. Golfers rest content with an unfinished argument about the weight and size of the ball. Rugby football sometimes regurgitates an ancient question concerning the points-value of a dropped goal. Association has flirted with the notion of one referee for each half of the field. But neither code has so far proposed that a match should consist of 15 minutes play each way.

R C Robertson-Glasgow on suggestions of one-day cricket, *Wisden*, 1945

You cannot be a great fast bowler on a bottle of ginger pop.

Arthur Carr after being asked why Harold Larwood bowled his best after a couple of lunchtime pints

In order to slim, he drank cider, although the latter day dieticians might look askance at a GP supping scrumpy to reduce his waistline.

Eric Midwinter, *W G Grace*, 1981

We had different ideas of fitness. To me the best preparation for batting, bowling and fielding was batting, bowling and fielding.

Peter May, 1985

Despite his sociable temperament, Bill had to cut out the parties during the Test matches, and this contributed to the tension he was under.

Ralph Barker, *The Cricketing Family Edrich*, 1976

Hobbs, Hammond and Broad: it doesn't quite ring true, does it?

Chris Broad after he became the third Englishman to score three 100s on successive Tests against Australia in 1986

I was never coached; I was never told how to hold
a bat.

Don Bradman

When you see a cricket coach, run off as fast as you can.

Bill O'Reilly, Aussie spinner and journalist

There's a big difference between being fit and being strong. Sebastian Coe is fit, but he couldn't bowl all day.

Alec Bedser, 1993

I reckon you can't pull a muscle if you haven't got any.

John Emburey, 1989

During the winter I train on 20 fags and a couple of pints of lager and an unrelieved diet of cricket talk.

Brian Brain, 1981

Depends on how long out of bed I was. Could be 70 or 80 if I was up early enough.

Former Australian batsman Doug Walters on the average number of daily cigarettes he smoked during his career

Shane Warne's idea of a balanced diet is a cheeseburger in each hand.

Ian Healy, 1996

In my day 58 beers between London and Sydney would have virtually classified you as a teetotaller.

Ian Chappell on David Boon's alleged drinking record, 1989

I hate the helmets, the visors and the chest protectors. I would dearly love the boys to go out there like playboys, with a box, some gloves and a bat, play off the back foot and enjoy it.

Denis Compton, 1995

If someone had produced a batting helmet during the Bodyline series, I would certainly have worn it.

Don Bradman

I'll tell you what pressure is. Pressure is a
Messerschmitt up your arse. Playing
cricket is not.

Keith Miller

He is said to have frequently gone in to bat not
knowing his team's score, dropping his cards to grab
his cap and bat.

Jack Pollard on Dougie Walters,
***Australian Cricket*, 1982**

Fitness training consisted of lengthy games of
soccer between the capped and uncapped players.
Matches lasted as long at it took for the capped
players to win.

Ray East, *A Funny Turn*, 1983

We used to eat so many salads there was danger of
contracting myxomatosis.

Ray East, *A Funny Turn*, 1983

They're not bad this lot, but if we played 'em on
uncovered wickets we'd give 'em an innings start.

**Ray Illingworth offers grudging praise of Yorkshire's 2001
county championship winning side**

When I see a young man who has an expensive
and pretty hair-do, I have doubts as to his ability to
reach Test standard.

Ted Dexter

The golden age is behind us. But then it always was.

Benny Green

I absolutely insist that all my boys should be
in bed before breakfast.

**Hampshire captain Colin Ingleby-Mackenzie explains the
secret of his and Hampshire's success in 1961**

I'm glad they hadn't invented Spinvision in my day.
It would have shown the ball coming out straight.
I'd have been carted.

Vic Marks, 1995

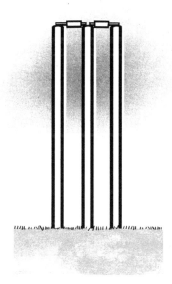

Bailey awoke from an apparent coma to strike a boundary.

P G Wodehouse on Trevor Bailey

I'm a big believer that the coach is something you travel in to get to and from the game.

Shane Warne with a dig at John Buchanan

YET MORE
LEGENDS OF
CRICKET

He didn't say much so you didn't know if he hated your guts.

Steve Waugh on Curtly Ambrose

I was interested to hear Michael Holding say that Curtly is still learning. I hope he doesn't learn too much more.

Alan Border on Curtly Ambrose, 1983

[Steve] Waugh's first hundred drained the life from his opponents. His second buried them. Mark Waugh is a rose to his brother's thorn.

Peter Roebuck after Steve Waugh's centuries in both innings in the 1997 Manchester Ashes Test

In Akram's hands a ball does not so much talk as sing. With a flick of the wrist and an arm that flashes past his ears like a thought through a child's brain he pushes the ball across the batsmen and makes it dip back wickedly late.

Peter Roebuck on Wasim Akram

As great a spinner as ever was born. He does things no one else even thinks about and he does them standing on his head.

Peter Roebuck on Shane Warne, 1994

Warne swaggered down the middle of the road, living large but always bowling big, revelling in the attention while never losing the love of his craft, seeming to treat the tabloid exposés as sixes hit off his bowling.

Just an occupational hazard.

Gideon Haigh, *On Warne*, 2012

In the space of one delivery so much
had changed. My confidence was sky-high.
I was pumped up and
rock 'n' rollin'.

**Shane Warne after his ball of the century to Gatting
in 1993**

Warne? He knew no such inhibition ...
he might have been bowling his first Test delivery
in a new country, in the biggest series of
his life, on a pitch presumed to be
unsympathetic, and at a hinge point
to boot; England were one for 80 chasing 289.
But Warne did not try simply to land it
thereabouts; he did not slide the ball out
to obtain a soothing dot; he surfed the wave
of his own adrenaline, and spun as hard
as he was able.

Gideon Haigh, *On Warne*, 2012

Gatting remained rooted at the crease for several seconds in disbelief rather than dissent – before trudging off to the pavilion like a man betrayed.

Vic Marks, *Wisden*, 1994

I suppose I can say 'I was there' at the moment he first indicated his potential to the wider world. There or thereabouts anyway.

Mike Gatting on being the victim of the ball of the century

He walks out to bat radiating as much intensity as someone toddling to the newsagent for the *Racing Post*.

Gideon Haigh on Damien Martyn

A heroic performance – really the stuff of which
schoolboy novels were made.

**Christopher Martin-Jenkins on Sachin Tendulkar's
maiden Test century in 1990**

Nothing bad can happen to us if we're on a plane in India with Sachin Tendulkar on it.

South African batsman Hashim Amla

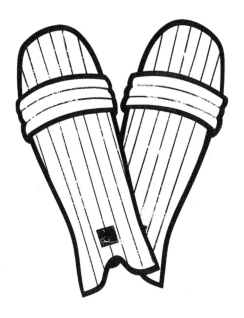

The archives recall not one incriminating
incident, not one drunken escapade, not one
reported affair, not one spat with a teammate
and reporter. As Matthew Parris wondered
of Barack Obama in these pages recently,
is he human?

**Mike Atherton on Sachin Tendulkar, *The Times*,
2008**

If Sachin bats well, India sleeps well.

Harsha Bhogle

He has been in form longer than some of
our guys have been alive.

Daniel Vettori on Sachin Tendulkar

I have seen God. He bats at No. 4
for India.

Matthew Hayden on Sachin Tendulkar

I do not think anyone can become God. I am a normal person who plays cricket.

Sachin Tendulkar

Tendulkar has carried the burden of the nation for 21 years. It is time we carried him on our shoulders.

Virat Kohli leads the Tendulkar tributes after India's World Cup triumph

I can imagine cricket without Sachin, but I can't imagine Sachin without cricket.

Sachin Tendulkar's wife, Anjali, on her husband's retirement, 2013

He destroys bowlers nicely.

Bob Woolmer on Brian Lara

Pietersen would be deemed brash by a Texan assertiveness coach.

Simon Wilde on KP, *Sunday Times*

Pietersen is the most fascinating of the present crop of batsmen, and I suspect he would say the same.

Mike Atherton

I watched every ball and I've never seen anyone as
disinterested or distracted on a cricket
field as Kevin. It led me to talk to every person
on the management team within England
and a lot outside it. I also talked to quite
a few senior players and couldn't find one
supporter who said 'we want KP to stay in
the side'.

**Paul Downton, briefly ECB managing director, on his
controversial decision to sack Kevin Pietersen from the
England team in 2014**

In team meetings during the tour, KP would
often be deliberately disengaged (e.g. looking
out of the window, looking at his watch etc.
whilst AF and others were talking to
the team).

**Extract from the secret ECB dossier produced
after the 2013/14 Ashes tour to explain why Pietersen
was sacked**

You can be an individual within the team but you cannot just be an individual. He has said this is how I play take it or leave it, well they've taken it for long enough and now they've said thank you very much, we will leave it.

Geoff Boycott on KP's sacking

It's tough being me.

Kevin Pietersen

I had to ask if he was a batter or a bowler – I didn't really know who he was.

Liberty X singer Jessica Taylor on fiancé Kevin Pietersen

Kohli killed us softly . . .

New Zealand coach Mike Hesson on Virat Kohli's double-hundred against his side, 2016

Virat Kohli is the Prince of Indian cricket.

Ian Chappell

A B is like a mind-reading bloodhound. He can smell the emotions of the opposition and he predicts what they are going to do and how they will behave.

Dale Steyn waxes lyrical about the prodigious talent of his teammate, A B de Villiers

THE
MODERN
GAME

I really get annoyed with this reverse swing term. It's
either an outswinger or an inswinger, isn't it?

Ian Chappell

There has been speculation it [night cricket] might
be introduced in England on regular basis. At
present this appears unlikely; our climate is less
accommodating; in mid-summer the sun refuses to
set, at autumn the dew falls and rumour has it that
there are one or two MCC members who would
question the wisdom of erecting half a dozen massive
pillars around our sacred headquarters at Lord's.

For once, Vic Marks' crystal ball appears to be faulty,
***Barclays World Of Cricket*, 1986**

Cricket must be the only business where you can
make more money in one day than in three.

Pat Gibson

The next thing you know, they'll be wanting to play
with a ball with a bell in it.

**Alec Bedser was unimpressed with the introduction of
floodlit cricket during the Packer Revolution**

The dot ball has become the Holy Grail.

Colin Cowdrey, 1982

One-day cricket is like fast food. No one wants to cook.

Viv Richards

It's like Manchester United getting a penalty and
Bryan Robson taking it with his head.

**David Lloyd on the reverse sweep; he's since
changed his mind …**

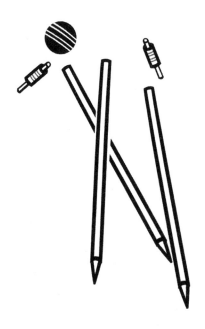

We came to play cricket but lost at skittles.

Alan Igglesden after Kent lost a bowl out in 1994

When I first started they put the beers on ice. Now they put the players on ice.

Darren Lehmann

In my playing days the ice was kept for the beers.

Michael Holding looks askance at modern post-match routines

Dawyne Leverock is the physical embodiment of the World Cup's new format: vast and overblown.

Harry Pearson

The days of women's cricket being seen as a knicker
parade must be over.

**Norman Izard, manager of England women's 1993 World
Cup winning side**

I couldn't
have played
that shot
and I'm
left-handed.

**David Gower on Kevin Pietersen's switch
hit shot**

When I first joined Middlesex there was a big cards school when it rained ... now, with all the public schoolboys in the Middlesex team, they play Scrabble.

Mark Ramprakash

Twenty20 is good for the game but not for the ego.

Andrew Symonds after being hit for 16 off three balls to lose his IPL side the game

The hardest part about the whole affair was that it took me a month to get the fake tan off my hand.

Simon Katich talks about the time he grabbed Michael Clarke by the throat in a post-match contretemps

There are 10,000 people in that stadium and 3,000 of them will be overweight … Freddie has become a role model for them.

Andrew Flintoff's agent 'Chubby' Chandler sums up his man's popularity in 2000

There's no secret we had a few drinks … there was water involved and a pedalo as well. But I don't think my life was in danger.

England all-rounder Andrew Flintoff on his late-night drinking binge at the 2007 World Cup

Start the car, launch the pedalo.

David Lloyd gets very excited as Steve Harmison takes two quick wickets on the final day at Old Trafford; Andrew Flintoff was watching from the England balcony

I lost the World Cup. Nobody died.

A philosophical Lance Klusener after his and Alan Donald's run out cost South Africa the semi final against Australia at the 1999 World Cup

I started the day crying, and I finished the day crying.

Nicky Shaw, Player of the Match, 2009 Women's World Cup final

The monkey's almost become a gorilla now and
until we win an ICC event it's always going to be
there I'm afraid.

**Mickey Arthur admits the pressure is piling up on South
Africa to break their World Cup jinx**

He would rather go to bed early and read a book on
sports psychology.

**Dave Houghton says that the ECB has no need to worry
that their new assistant coach Andy Flower will go out
drinking with the England team**

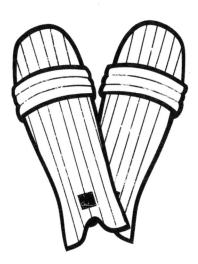

I saw only two murders in the theatre, but ended up watching many more during the Ireland-England game.

Munaf Patel left Bollywood movie *Saat Khoon Maaf* ('Forgive Seven Murders'), halfway through to see Kevin O'Brien and Ireland shock England in the 2011 World Cup

Certainly I am told that you can play cricket better after a marijuana cigarette than after a couple of pints of beer.

Old Bailey judge Basil Wigoder

I am very happy and it will allow me to have lot more rice.

Eoin Morgan's reaction to being given a rice cooker as a Man of the Match award, 2013

Tough times don't last, but tough blokes do.

Brendon McCullum on Eoin Morgan, 2015

The only thing that seems to be in
common is they've got wood and they've
got a grip.

**Barry Richards on the difference between old and new
cricket bats, 2015**

A big boy
needs a big bat.

**Chris Gayle gives his considered opinion on
modern bats, 2015**

Getting a hundred in 31 balls was unheard of. I took
31 balls to get off the mark.

Sunil Gavaskar on the modern one-day game, 2015

It might be just three hours, but an IPL game is a
condensed scripture on cricket. Timeless.

Ravi Shastri, 2015

He seemed to have used copious amounts more red
wine ...

**Jos Buttler on how Ian Botham's Test match preparation
differs from the modern player, 2015**

You are a jerk! I averaged two ...

**Glenn Maxwell tweets a response to a critic who wrote that he
only averaged one in an ODI series against New Zealand, 2016**

You can't exactly put a fielder in the car park, can you?

Ravi Bopara on the problems of containing Chris Gayle, 2016

It's like kissing your brother, I guess.

South Africa women's captain Dane van Niekerk's unique view on how it feels to tie a match, 2016

It smells a lot different.

England batsman Sarah Taylor on the differences between a male and female dressing room, 2016

GAFFES
AND
GAGS

You've come over at a very appropriate time.
Ray Illingworth has just relieved himself at the
Pavilion End.

Brian Johnston

The last bowler to be knighted was Sir Francis Drake.

**Former spinner Arthur Mailey on hearing Len Hutton, a
batsman, had been given a knighthood, 1956**

Imagine if you got him on a triple word score in
Scrabble!

**David Lloyd on Warnakulasuriya Patabendige Ushantha
Joseph Chaminda Vaas (aka Chaminda Vaas)**

Trueman threw his balls down with ferocity.

Los Angeles Times, 1964

Damn fool brought out my
reading glasses!

**Actor C Aubrey Smith after he had called for his butler
to bring him his spectacles to help his fielding, and then
dropped a dolly**

Watching Clinton steal a match in which Hick and Botha are playing is like going to a Pavarotti concert and seeing him upstaged by Des O'Connor.

Mike Selvey, *The Guardian*, May 1989

You know that summer has arrived when you hear the sound of leather on Brian Close.

Eric Morecambe

I had an extra pray and asked Allah to give us another championship.

Mushtaq Ahmed on Sussex's second title win in 2006

I would like to thank Allah too because he's clearly played his part.

Sussex captain Chris Adams backs up Ahmed's faith

I was a bit concerned my name wasn't going to fit on the shirt.

Ebony-Jewel Cora-Lee Camellia Rosamond Rainford-Brent

Merv Hughes.

Steve Waugh's answer to the question, 'What's your favourite animal?'

And Glenn McGrath dismissed for two, just 98 runs short of his century.

Richie Benaud

To be honest, Mark, I'm struggling.

A tired and emotional Freddie Flintoff to Mark Nicholas the morning after England's momentous 2005 Ashes win

Neil Harvey's at slip, his legs wide apart, waiting for
a tickle.

Brian Johnston

It's going to be Snow to the crouching Henry Horton
who looks like he's shitting, er, sitting on a
shooting stick.

Brian Johnston, 1967

I'm joined by the Balls, er, I mean the Boil.

Brian Johnston

England have nothing to lose here, apart from this Test match.

David Lloyd

Anyone foolish enough to predict the outcome of
this match is a fool.

Fred Trueman

Cricket is indescribable. How do you describe an orgasm?

Greg Matthews

Like an elephant trying to do the pole vault.

Jonathan Agnew describing Inzamam-ul-Haq's futile and ungainly attempts to avoid being dismissed hit wicket

'You must have put a few spectators to sleep in your time, Geoffrey?'
'Yeah, but I were still battin' when they woke up!'

Exchange between Simon Mann and Geoff Boycott on *TMS* in 2011

'He's been feng shui'd.'
'What do you mean, feng shui'd?'
'Had his furniture rearranged.'

Phil Tufnell teaches Christopher Martin-Jenkins a new cricket term, after seeing Matt Prior clean bowled by Mitchell Johnson, 2009

Goodbye from Southampton and now over to
Edgbaston for some more balls from Rex Alston.

John Arlott

Yorkshire 232 all out. Hutton ill. No, I'm sorry –
Hutton III.

John Snagge, 1946

Bill Frindall has done a bit of mental arithmetic with
a calculator.

John Arlott

Yes, he just didn't quite get his leg over …

**Jonathan Agnew's infamous comment about Ian Botham's
hit-wicket dismissal in 1991, which prompted him and
Brian Johnston to corpse live on air**

Michael Vaughan is beside me. It's not easy
putting a rubber on, is it?

**Jonathan Agnew, watching Kevin Pietersen change
the grip on his bat, 2011**

Closest sport in America is baseball. But
cricket lasts five days. We break every now
and then for food. And we spend
a lot of time rubbing our balls on
our trousers.

**Andrew Flintoff tries gamely to explain cricket to
Jennifer Lopez, 2013**

In the rear, the small diminutive figure
of Shoaib Mohammad, who can't be much taller
than he is.

Henry Blofeld

In Australia they think I'm Stephen Hawking.

**Andrew Flintoff on his new role presenting
a current affairs programme Down
Under, 2015**

Some days you're the windscreen, some you're the bug.

Michael Hussey on cricket's vicissitudes, 2012

A bit of sunburn, probably, to be honest

**Ben Stokes on what England could take away from
a tough day in the field against India, 2015**

They are still in a Diwali mood. They keep giving gifts.

Sunil Gavaskar after India dropped numerous chances against England in Rajkot, 2015

CLOSE
OF
PLAY

When an old cricketer leaves the crease, you never
know whether he's gone,
If sometimes you're catching a fleeting glimpse of a
twelfth man at silly mid-on,
And it could be Geoff and it could be John with a
new ball sting in his tail,
And it could be me and it could be thee and
it could be the sting in the ale,
Sting in the ale.

Roy Harper, 'When an Old Cricketer Leaves the Crease'

After all, every good thing must come to an end.
And the end ought to come when failures begin to
affect you more than successes, as they have done in
my case this season.

Jack Hobbs during his final Test against Australia, 1933

I'm going while you still ask why. I'm not waiting
until you ask why not.

Patsy Hendren explains his retirement

And what do you say under those circumstances?
I wonder if you see the ball very clearly in your
last Test in England? On a ground where you've
played some of the biggest cricket of your life
and where the opposing side has just stood
around you and given you three cheers,
and the crowd has clapped you all the way
to the wicket – I wonder if you really see the
ball at all?

**John Arlott on Don Bradman's last Test innings at the
Oval in 1948**

Endless cricket, like endless anything else, simply
grinds you down.

Ted Dexter on retirement

I used to bowl tripe, then I wrote it, now I sell it.

**The words written on Arthur Mailey's butcher's
shop near Sydney**

I've had about ten operations. I'm a bit like
a battered old Escort. You might find one panel left
that's an original.

Ian Botham at the end of his career

The realisation that time is tapping you on the
shoulder doesn't creep up on you, it literally swamps
you overnight.

Mike Atherton on retirement

I wouldn't enjoy making my living by criticising my
former colleagues.

**Bob Willis delivers his verdict on players turned pundits,
1983; he has gone on to make a living as a stern critic of
modern cricketers**

When I walk off the field for the last time –
whenever that will be – it will be with an enormous
sense of relief.

Barry Richards, 1978

All I got after 15 years at the club was a cup of coffee
in the chief executive's office.

Matthew Hoggard on leaving Yorkshire

When he asked me if I wanted to turn out, I thought
he wanted me to play him at golf.

**Fred Titmus after being recalled to the Middlesex side aged
46, via a phone call from secretary Don Bennett**

You think my
run up was
long. Now you
should hear my
speeches.

**Wes Hall, former West Indies quick bowler, who became a
politician in Barbados, 1987**

So great was his own love for the game that, at 70, he still had an occasional bowl in his garden, but was heard to say that he had lost some of his pace from the pitch.

Ian Peebles on the great Aussie leg-spinner Clarrie Grimmett, *Barclays World of Cricket*, 1986

Just think. All those physios I'm putting out of work.

The often-injured Graham Dilley on his retirement in 1992

You should play every game as if it's your last, but make you perform well enough to ensure that it's not.

John Emburey

The game you are frightened of losing is not worth winning.

Benny Green

I see they've got you down at third man again, old man.

Arthur Milton on seeing the grave of his old teammate Sam Cook in a far-flung corner of the churchyard

I'm very well and don't even need Viagra,

even at 78.

Farokh Engineer confirms he is alive and well after rumours of his death in 2016

If anyone had told me in 1994 that I would play 100 Tests for my country, I would have asked them what they were smoking.

Gary Kirsten at the end of his career, 2004

It's going to be really hard not going to breakfast with a miserable Jimmy Anderson every morning, breaking him in slowly through the day and seeing a smile about teatime.

Graeme Swann on what he'd miss most after retirement, 2013

I would most like to thank the opposition batters who somehow for over a decade missed the straight ones and nicked the half-volleys ... to you all I'll be forever grateful.

Hampshire seamer James Tomlinson offers a heartfelt tribute and thanks on his retirement, 2016

The next time I retire will be the last time.

Shahid Afridi, 2011

Hyland, Frederick J. who died in February, aged 70, played as a professional in one match for Hampshire in 1924. Cricket in this game, in Northampton, was limited by rain to two overs from which Northamptonshire scored one run without loss. Hyland later earned a reputation as a nurseryman in Cheshire.

Wisden, **1965, pays tribute to a singular and brief first-class career**

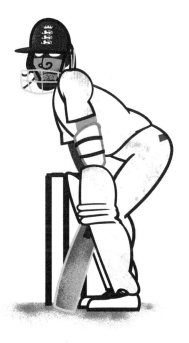

For the field is full of shades as I near the shadowy coast

And a ghostly batsman plays to the bowling

of a ghost

And I look through my tears on a

soundless-clapping host

As the run stealers flicker to and fro

To and fro:

O My Hornby and my Barlow long ago!

Francis Thompson, 'At Lord's'

BIBLIOGRAPHY

Specific sources are cited throughout the text but the following publications and websites also proved enormously helpful in compiling this book.

Benson, Richard, *Cricket Wit*, Summersdale, 2013

Booth, Lawrence, *What are the Butchers For?* John Wisden & Co Ltd, 2009

Holt, Nick, *The Wit and Wisdom of Cricket*, Prion, 2012

Hopps, David, *Great Cricket Quotes*, Robson, 2006

Johnston, Barry, *The Wit of Cricket*, Hodder & Stoughton, 2009

Lemmon, David, *The Wisden Book of Cricket Quotations*, Queen Anne Press, 1990

Rosenwater, Irving, *500 Notable Cricket Quotations*, Andre Deutsch, 1996

www.espncricinfo.com
www.guardian.co.uk
www.independent.co.uk
www.telegraph.co.uk
www.thetimes.co.uk

ACKNOWLEDGEMENTS

I'd like to thank Bethany Wright and Yvonne Jacob at Ebury for all their help. Many thanks also to Marina De Pass and my agent Araminta Whitley at LAW for their invaluable advice and assistance.

I'm also very grateful to Neil Robinson and Robert Curphey at the MCC Library for allowing me to make use of their well-stocked bookshelves.

INDEX

Aaron, Varun 112
Acfield, David 66
Adams, Chris 298
Afridi, Shahid 318
Agnew, Jonathan
  on changing the grip 305
  on Botham's dismissal 304
  on Cook's mutterings 152
  on Derby 182, 183
  on Harmison's delivery 138
  on his nickname 253
  on Inzamam-ul-Haq 303
Ahmed, Mushtaq 298
Akram, Waqar 129
Akram, Wasim 69, 129, 269
Ali, Moeen 223
All on a Summer's Day (Hughes) 84, 237
All Round View (Khan) 109
Ambrose, Curtly 61, 268
Amla, Hashim 273
Anderson, Jimmy 317
Another Bloody Day in Paradise (Keating)
  42, 43, 60, 248
Anyone But England (Marqusee) 117
Arlott, John
  on batting 37
  on Bradman's last Test 311
  on Compton's late stroke 34
  on Clive Lloyd 35, 249
  on Dexter's bowling 35
  on Dickie Bird and rain 108
  on D'Oliveira affair 118
  Dylan Thomas on 241
  on England win over South
    Africa 254
  on fielders 253
  on 'freakers' 240
  gags 304
  on gulls 249
  on Henry Moore sculpture 35
  on Hobbs's batting 72
  on Ian Chappell 154
  on Johnston 243

  on Kanhai's batting 35
  Keating on 242
  on lack of playing 243
  on Lillee 53
  on Loader hat-trick 58
  on Mann and Mann 57
  on Masood's run up 58
The Art of Captaincy (Brearley) 97
Arthur, Mickey 290
The Ashes 195–216
  1902 173
  1932/33 199, 200
  1946/47 50
  1953 251
  1954/55 202
  1968 32
  1973/74 37
  1974/75 141, 203, 204
  1975 31
  1981 205–7
  1986/87 208
  1989 208, 209
  1990/91 68, 186
  1994 210
  1994/95 186
  1997 212, 269
  2005 142, 212–15, 299
  2006/07 138, 142
  2009 216
  2013 133, 216
  2013/14 133, 216, 278
  2015 216
The Ashes Captain (Cotter) 1989
Ashes to Ashes (Roebuck) 162
"At Lord's" (Thompson) 319
Atherton, Mike
  on Benaud's commentary 252
  on ball tampering 124
  on concentration 170
  Fraser on 31
  on Illingworth's opinion of May 91
  on Merv Hughes' sledging 211
  on Pietersen's self-opinion 277

on retirement 312
and Russell as rear-guard 43
on The Spirit of Cricket 132
and Taj Mahal 218
on Tendulkar as not human 274
World Twenty20 192
Australian Cricket (Pollard) 263
Autobiography (Cardus) 78

bad light 108, 245
Background of Cricket (Gordon) 256
Bailey, Trevor 202, 234, 266
Bairstow, David 42, 148, 182
ball-tampering 124, 128, 129
Barclays World of Cricket (Swanton)
      75, 84, 139, 154, 169, 282, 315
Barker, Ralph 258
Barlow, Eddie 92
Barmy Army 254
Barnes, S F 51
Barnes, Simon 213, 220, 226
Barnes, Sydney 75, 76, 99
Barrington, Ken 147, 173
Bat and Ball (Moult) 17
batsmen 27–46
Bayliss, Trevor 216
Bedi, Bishan 69, 70
Bedser, Alec 79, 128, 260, 283
Benaud, Richie
      Atherton on 252
      on batting 33
      on Botham's batting 205, 206
      on captaincy 94
      on McGrath's two runs 299
      to Meckiff 123
      on streakers 252
Benitez, Rafa 12
Bentine, Michael 253
Berkmann, Marcus 21, 23, 24, 164
Berry, Scyld 167, 246
Best Loved Game (Moorhouse) 20
Between Wickets (Robinson) 33
Beyond a Boundary (James) 14
Bhogle, Harsha 241, 275
Bird, Dickie 107–8
Birley, Derek 219
Blofeld, Henry
      on Botham's skill 160
      on buses 250
      on Close's batting 89
      on cricket management 191
      on England loss to Zimbabwe 224
      on Graves 194

on limping butterfly 250
on Shoaib Mohammad 306
Blunden, Edmund 10
Bodyline 112, 141, 198, 199, 201, 262
Bolus, Brian 103
Book of Cricketers (Arlott) 72
Boon, David 261
Booth, Lawrence 22, 119, 126, 244
Bopara, Ravi 294
Border, Alan 166, 209, 268
Bose, Mihir 116
Boswell, Scott 131
Botham, Ian
      The Ashes 205, 206, 207
      Blofeld on 160
      Close on 102
      on Dickie Bird 107
      first ball after suspension 160
      on Gatting affair 165
      on his reputation 161
      and Ian Chappell 253
      Keating on slow ball 54
      on nappy-changing 160
      and Pakistan 223
      preparation 293
      Roebuck on 161
      Selvey on 298
      on surgery 312
      Trueman on 138
bouncers 50
Bowes, Bill 201
bowlers 29, 47–70
Bowling 'em out (Verity) 56
Boycott, Geoff
      on batting 28, 43
      on Bradman's batting 157
      Brearley on 156
      to Cameron 152
      on Daniel Radcliffe 151
      Engel on 156
      on failed catch 151
      on Gatting being selected 186
      on getting out 156
      on girls' hockey 150
      on his mum 150
      on Jesus 155
      Keating on 60
      Kelner on documentary 158
      Martin-Jenkins, Christopher on 158
      on McGrath 60
      on Pietersen's sacking 279
      Root on 46
      on runs 164

Boycott, Geoff (*continued*)
  on spectators 303
  Trueman on 158, 251
  on Underwood 65
  walking on water 148
  on Waqar and Wasim Akram 129
Bracewell, John 31
Bradman, Don
  on The Ashes 196
  on batsmen and bowlers 28
  Bedser on 79
  on Bodyline series 262
  Boycott on 157
  Cardus on 78, 79
  East on 70
  Engel on 156
  Hobbs on 80
  Kilburn on 82
  on lack of coaching 259
  Laker on 78
  Larwood on 80
  last Test 311
  on McCabe's batting 38
  Robertson-Glasgow on 81
  Stackpole on 81
Brain, Brian 260
Brearley, Mike
  on Boycott 156
  captaincy 97, 100
  on cricket 114
  on Ian Chappell 155
  letter to *Guardian* about 246
  on the press 247
  umpire to 110
Broad, Chris 259
Broad, Stuart 64, 133
Bryson, Bill 121
Buchanan, John 152, 266
Burke, Jimmy 122
Buttler, Joe 293

Cameron, David 152
The Canberra Times 227
Canterbury tree 191
captaincy 93–104
Captaincy (Illingworth) 96
Cardus, Neville
  on Australians 219
  on Bradman 78, 79
  on C B Fry meeting Hitler 83
  on cricket 12, 15, 17, 118
  on Hobbs 72, 73
  on Lord's 236

  on Robinson's bowling 50
  on Sobers 89
  on umpires 106
  on wicket 232, 233
Carey, Michael 184
Carr, Arthur 82, 257
centenary test, Melbourne 1977 37
Champions Trophy 152
Chandler, 'Chubby' 288
Chappell, Greg 39, 126, 210
Chappell, Ian
  Arlott on 154
  and Botham 253
  Brearley on 155
  on drinking records 261
  on England 172
  on Kohli 280
  Marlar on 154
  on reverse swing 282
  on Tufnell's bowling 68
Chappell, Trevor 124
Chester, Frank 112
Clarke, Michael 112, 152, 287
Clinton, Grahame 298
Close, Brian
  on bowlers 30
  Blofeld on 89
  on Botham's captaincy 102
  East on 140
  on fast bowlers 54
  Greig on 221
  Morecambe and Wise joke 298
  on Yorkshire 89, 180
Coldham, James P 181
The Complete Cricketer (Knight) 98
Compton, Denis 33, 34, 86, 87,
    262
Connor, Clare 176
Constantine, Sir Learie 32, 88
Conway, Doug 227
Cook, Alastair 45, 152, 216
Cook, Jimmy 46
Cook, Sam 316
Cook, Stephen 46
Cooke, Alistair 25
Cotter, Gerry 73
Cottey, Tony 146
Cowdrey, Chris 144
Cowdrey, Colin 203, 283
Cox, Geoffrey 245
Crawford, Michael 179
Cricket – The Great Ones (Arlott) 84
Cricket on the Brain (Hollowood) 75

Cricket Characters (Martin-Jenkins)
 61, 158, 166
Cricket Decade (Kilburn) 13
Cricket Heroes (Frith) 88
Cricket Lovely Cricket (Booth) 11, 22,
 119, 126
Cricket Prints (Robertson-Glasgow) 86, 95
Cricket Society 181
The Cricketer 245
The Cricketing Family Edrich
 (Barker) 258
Cricket's Second Golden Age (Howat)
 88, 221
Cricket's Unholy Trinity (Foot) 131, 233, 244
Crusoe on Cricket (Robertson-
 Glasgow) 112

The Daily Express 162
The Daily Mail 228, 229
Dalton, Alastair 146
Darling, Joe 99
Davis, Michael 167
De Villiers, A B 280
Denis Compton: A Cricket Sketch
 (Swanton) 20
Denness, Mike 141, 143
Dev, Kapil 61, 219
Dexter, Ted 35, 183, 186, 202, 264, 311
Dilley, Graham 205, 206, 315
Dobell, George 194
D'Oliveira, Basil 118
Donald, Alan 289
Donald Duck 70
Dorset, Duke of 13
Downton, Paul 278
Dredge, Colin 229
du Plessis, Faf 104

East, Ray 70, 140, 263, 264
Edmonds, Frances 143, 162, 185
Edmonds, Phil 55, 66, 143
Edrich, Bill 86, 258
Eeyore 49
An Eighteenth Century View of Cricket
 (Gutsmuths) 18
Emburey, John 146, 148, 222, 260, 315
Engel, Matthew 109, 156, 169, 188, 190,
 191, 248
Engineer, Farokh 316
The English (Priestley) 83
English Social History (Trevelyan) 14
Evans, Godfrey 50
An Eye for Cricket (Arlott) 37, 154

Farewell to Cricket (Bradman) 196
fast bowling 35, 54, 55, 57, 62, 89, 127
Fast Fury (Trueman) 114
Father Christmas 204
Fernando, Ranjit 53
Ferriday, Patrick 69
Fingleton, Jack 10
Flashman's Lady (MacDonald
 Fraser) 234
Fletcher, Duncan 145, 213
Fletcher, Keith 101, 102, 187
Flintoff, Andrew (Freddie) 215, 288,
 289, 299, 306
floodlit cricket 283
Flower, Andy 290
Flower, Andy and Olonga, Henry 228
Foot, David 131, 233
Fowler, Graeme 53
Fraser, Angus 31, 49, 57
Fred Trueman's Book of Cricket 114
Frindall, Bill 304
Frith, David 88, 91
Fry, C B 75, 83
Fry, Stephen 136
Fulton, David 132
A Funny Turn (East) 140, 263, 264

Gatting, Mike
 and ball of century from Warne 67,
  271, 272
 Boycott on 186
 on cricket 127
 on demonstration in South Africa 125
 and food 144, 165
 on Hadlee's bowling 159
 Marks on 272
Gavaskar, Sunil 145, 167, 245, 293, 308
Gayle, Chris 292, 294
Genghis Khan 123
Gibson, Pat 283
Giffen, George 42
Gilbert, Dave 191
Giles, Ashley 65, 251
Gillespie, Jason 212
Gillette Cup 108
Golden Age of cricket 72, 78, 264
golf 34, 257, 314
Gooch, Graham 102, 104, 160, 165, 169,
 186, 209
Good Days (Cardus) 12, 106, 232
Gordon, Sir Home 256
Gough, Darren 44, 100, 139
Gould, Ian 112

Gower, David
    on Australian lack of culture 216
    on batting 36, 43
    on fast bowling 127
    on Gatting 144
    Johnson on 210
    as laid back 162
    leaves press conference 208
    on Pietersen 286
    resignation 128
    Roebuck on 162
Grace, W G
    on batsmen 39
    as Beethoven of cricket 73
    as captain 101
    on cricket 24
    importance of 74
    Kortright to 56
    slimming tactic 258
Graveney, Tom 92
Graves, Colin 194
Graves, Robert 115
Green, Benny 139, 264, 315
Greenidge, Gordon 143
Greig, Tony 221
Grimmett, Clarrie 82, 315
Grout, Wally 173
The Guardian 158, 214, 242, 246, 298
Gutsmuths, Johan 18

Hadlee, Richard 128, 159
Haigh, Gideon 21, 67, 164, 203, 270,
    271, 272
Hair, Darrell 124
Hall, Wes 227, 314
Hammond, Wally 41, 84, 85, 259
Hannibal 81
Hardy, J H 17
Harmison, Steve 138, 289
Harold Gimblett (Foot) 131
Harper, Roy 310
Harris, Lord 196, 234
Harvey, Neil 88, 300
Hawke, Lord 96, 139, 175
Hayden, Matthew 227, 275
Headley, George 77
Healy, Ian 261
Hendren, Patsy 310
Hesson, Mike 280
Heyhoe Flint, Rachael 174, 177
Hick, Graeme 31, 190, 298
Hirst, George 77
A History of Yorkshire Cricket (Kilburn) 87

Hobbs, Jack 41, 72, 73, 80, 259, 310
Hogg, Rodney 103
Hoggard, Matthew 63, 142, 213, 215, 313
Hoggard, Sarah 142
Holding, Michael 60, 89, 128, 221, 268, 285
Hollis, Christopher 20
Hollowood, Bernard 75, 76
Hookes, David 139
Hopps, David 148
Horton, Henry 300
Hotten, Jon 22, 130, 131
Houghton, Dave 290
Howat, Gerald 88, 221
Hughes, Kim 207
Hughes, Margaret 84, 237
Hughes, Merv 59, 211
Hughes, Simon 52, 102, 145, 159, 246
Hughes, Thomas 19
Hussain, Nasser 100, 212
Hussey, Mike 44, 307
Hutton, Len 11, 85, 116, 174, 180
Hutton, Richard 88
Hutton and the Past in Cricket (Pinter) 86
Hyland, Frederick J. 318

Igglesden, Alec 285
Illingworth, Ray
    on captaincy 96
    on cricket 19
    Engel on 191
    Frith on 91
    Johnston gag 296
    Lewis on 90
    on Lord MacLaurin 178
    on May 91
    on the press 247
    on Yorkshire 264
In It to Win It (Roebuck) 197
The Independent 182, 245
Ingleby-Mackenzie, Colin 101, 265
Insole, Doug 99, 147
Inzamam-ul-Haq 223, 303
It Never Rains (Roebuck) 95, 119, 120
Izard, Norman 286

James, C L R 14
Jardine, Douglas
    Aussie fans to 141, 198
    on captaincy 97
    on cricket 19, 25
    to the Nawab of Pataudi 201
    Wilson on 199
    and Yorkshire 179

Jarmusch, Jim 121
Jephson, D L A 177
Jepson, Arthur 108
Jerry, Michael Clarke's dog 152
Jessop, Gilbert 29
Johnson, Martin
  on The Ashes 208, 209, 210
  on Gatting and 'ball of the century' 67
  on Hick 190
  on Merv Hughes 59
  on preparation for test match 182
  on Willey 149
Johnson, Mitchell 46, 303
Johnston, Brian 243, 296, 300, 301, 304
Jones, Simon 62, 63
The Jubilee Book of Cricket (Prince
  Ranjitsinhji) 74, 238

Kanhai, Rohan 35
Katich, Simon 287
Keating, Frank
  on Arlott's voice 242
  on Botham's slow ball 54
  on bowling 60
  on England win 42
  on Gower's appearance 162
  on Graveney 92
  on journalists 248
  on Willis as bowler 49
Kelner, Martin 158
Kerr, Bernard 251
Key, Rob 46
Khan, Imran 109, 169, 225
Kilburn, J M
  on Bradman's batting 82
  on cricket 13
  on Graveney 92
  on Hammond's importance 84
  on Lord's 236
  on Trueman's greatness 87
Kilner, Roy 77, 143
Kippax, A F 33
Kirsten, Gary 317
Klusener, Lance 289
Knight, A E 98
Knott, Alan 175
Kohli, Virat 276, 280
Kortright, Charles 56

Laker, Jim 51, 78, 197
Lamb, Lindsay 175
Lara, Brian 57, 140, 276
Larwood, Harold 48, 80, 82, 201, 257

Lawry, Bill 32
Lehmann, Darren 285
Lette, Kath 26
Leverock, Dwayne 285
Lewis, Tony 86, 90, 94
Leyland, Maurice 57, 86
Lillee, Dennis 37, 52, 53, 203, 204, 207
Lindwall, Ray 54
Lloyd, Clive 35, 52, 203, 249
Lloyd, David
  on batting 37
  on Johnston's commentary 243
  on England loss 224, 301
  on pedaloes 289
  on raffles 144
  on reverse sweep 284
  on Scrabble 296
Loader, Peter 58
Lock, Tony 147
Lord's
  benefit collection 246
  Bishop Tutu at 135
  defeat and ignominy 192
  gatemen 149
  or option of Raquel Welch 28
  The Queen 176
  uniqueness 234–8, 282
Lords 1946–1970 (Kerr and Peebles) 87
The Los Angeles Times 297
A Lot of Hard Yakka (Hughes) 159
Lovelace, Linda 26

MacDonald Fraser, George 234
Maclaren, A C 173
MacLaurin, Ian 178
Mailey, Arthur 82, 296, 311
Major, Sir John 16
Malcolm, Devon 50, 186
Mallet, Ashley 110
Mandela, Nelson 21
Mann, George 57
Mann, Simon 303
Mann, Tufty 57
Marks, Vic 106, 265, 272, 282
Marlar, Robin 154, 176
Marqusee, Mike 117
Marsh, Rod 184
Marshall, Howard 240
Marshall, Malcolm 70
Martin-Jenkins, Christopher
  on The Ashes 216
  on Boycott's character 158
  compares Border to a dog 166

Martin-Jenkins, Christopher (*continued*)
  compares Dev to a wild animal 61
  on feng shui 303
  on Tendulkar's heroism 273
  on Richards as uncrowned King 168
Martyn, Damien 272
Marx, Groucho 58, 204
Masood, Asif 58
Masterly Batting (Ferriday) 69
Matthews, Greg 302
Maxwell, Glenn 293
May, Peter 91, 97, 185, 258
McCabe, Stan 38
McCool, Colin 149
McCullum, Brendon 292
McGrath, Glen 59, 60, 299
The Meaning of Cricket (Hotten)
  22, 130, 131
Meckiff, Ian 'Dad' 123
Miandad, Javed 222
Midwinter, Eric 74, 258
Milburn, Colin 33, 34
Miller, Keith 50, 100, 263
Milton, Arthur 316
Mitchell, Kevin 155
Mohammad, Shoaib 306
Moody, Tom 189
Moore, Glen 245
Moore, Henry 35
Moorhouse, Geoffrey 20, 169
Morecambe, Eric 298
Morgan, Eoin 291, 292
Morgan, Piers 142
Moult, Thomas 17
Mugabe, Robert 25
Muldoon, Robert 124
Muralitharan, Muttiah 124
Murphy, Patrick 70
Murray, John 60

Nash, Malcolm 90
Nawab of Pataudi 201
Nelson, Fraser 136
Nicholas, Mark 61, 124

O'Brien, Kevin 291
The Observer on Cricket 122
Olonga, Henry 228
On and Off the Field (Smith) 41, 132
On Cricket (Parkinson) 22
On Warne (Haigh) 270, 271
one-day cricket 124, 131, 193, 257, 283,
  284, 293

O'Reilly, Bill 149, 260
Orwell, George 30, 117
The Oval 196, 213, 214, 216, 233, 236–7,
  311
Over to Me (Laker) 197
Overthrows (Kilburn) 236
Oxford Memories (Pycroft) 236

Packer, Kerry 123, 283
The Packer Revolution (Davis) 167
Parkinson, Michael 22, 36, 134, 143, 212
Patel, Munaf 291
Pearson, Harry 69, 285
Peebles, I A R 122, 315
Peebles, I A R and Kerr, Diana Rait 87
Peel, Robert 139
Pepper, Cec 110
Phelps, Stuart 146
Pietersen, Kevin 64, 213, 214, 277–9,
  286
Pinter, Harold 11, 86
Players v Gentlemen match 116
Playing Days (Lewis) 94
politics 118
Pollard, Jack 263
Pollock, Graeme 92
Ponting, Ricky 213
Pratt, Gary 213
Price, John 111
Priestley, J B 83, 226
Pringle, Derek 170
Prior, Matt 216, 303
Procter, Mike 103
Pycroft, Revd James 236

Qadir, Abdul 40
The Queen 176, 215

Rabada, Kagiso 104
Radcliffe, Daniel 151
rain 25, 108, 214, 244, 245, 287, 318
Rain Men (Berkmann) 23, 24, 164
Rainford-Brent, Ebony-Jewel Cora-Lee
  Camellia Rosamond 299
Ramprakash, Mark 287
Randall, Derek 37, 163
Ranjitsinhji, K S 28, 74, 238
Reed, Oliver 26
Reeve, Dermot 145, 146
refusal to walk 133
Reminiscences (Mailey) 296
Rhodes, Wilfred 34, 64, 72, 77, 119
Rice, Clive 125

Richards, Barry 220, 292, 313
Richards, Viv 66, 143, 167, 168, 284
Robertson-Glasgow, R C
  on Bradman's retirement 81
  on captaincy 95
  on Compton and Edrich as
    kings 86
  on Chester's umpiring 112
  on Headley's batting 77
  on Leyland 86
  on a missed catch 122
  on one-day cricket 257
  on The Oval and Lord's 237
  on Woolley's batting 78
Robinson, Emmott 50
Robinson, Ray 33
Roebuck, Peter
  on The Ashes 197
  on Border 166
  on Botham 161
  on captaincy 95
  Close to 30
  on cricket 119, 120, 121
  on Gower 162
  on Merv Hughes 59
  on Richards's batting 167
  on Steve Waugh 269
  on suicide 130
  on Warne's bowling 270
  on Wasim Akram 269
  on Yorkshire 182
Ronay, Barney 133
Root, Joe 46
Ross, Alan 134, 244
Russell, Jack 43

Sainsbury, Peter 64
Samuels, Marlon 149
Scott, Chris 140
Sehwag, Virender 36
Sellers, Brian 178
Selvey, Mike 49, 65, 148, 230, 298
Shastri, Ravi 293
Shaw, Nicky 289
Siddle, Peter 62
A Singular Man (Edmonds) 66
sledging 132, 137–52, 211
Slices of Cricket (Roebuck) 167
Smith, C Aubrey 297
Smith, Ed 41, 132
Smith, Giles 187, 189
Smyth, Rob 45
Snagge, John 304

Snow White 146
Sobers, Garry 89, 90, 247
spin bowling 64, 66, 67, 270–1
The Spinners Turn (Murphy) 70
Spofforth, Fred 42
Stackpole, Keith 81
Statham, Frank 51
Steel, Allan 'A G' Gibson 96
Steele, David 31, 204
Stevenson, Graeme 42
Stewart, Alec 57
Steyn, Dale 280
Sticky Wickets (Tennyson) 18
Stokes, Ben 307
streakers 240, 252
The Summer Game (Cardus) 236
The Sun 36, 126
The Sunday Times 277
Sutcliffe, Herbert 85
Swann, Graeme 193, 254, 317
Swanton, E W 'Jim' 20, 29, 176
The Sydney Morning Herald 212
Symonds, Andrew 287

Taj Mahal 218
Tangled Up in White (Roebuck) 130
Tavaré, Chris 164
Taylor, Clive 33
Taylor, Jessica (fiancée of Kevin
  Pietersen) 279
Taylor, Mark 43
Taylor, Mick 144
Taylor, Sarah 294
10 for 66 and All That (Mailey) 82
Tendulkar, Anjali 276
Tendulkar, Sachin 44, 62, 273–6
Tennyson, Lord 18
Thomas, Dylan 241
Thompson, Francis 319
Thomson, A A 97
Thomson, Jeff 37, 52, 53, 203, 204
The Times 132, 175, 189, 196, 226, 274
Titmus, Fred 147, 314
Tom Brown's Schooldays (Hughes) 19
Tomlinson, James 317
Trevelyan, G M 14
Troost, Andre van 229
Trueman, Fred
  on batting collapse 189
  on Botham's bowling 138
  on bowling 48
  bowling joke in press 297
  on Boycott 148, 158, 251

Trueman, Fred (*continued*)
    on colour TV 256
    on England 172
    on Gough's bowling 139
    Hutton on 88
    Kilburn on 87
    on predicting results 302
    on record for most Test wickets 87
    on the rules 114
    on Sainsbury's bowling 64
    on theorists 114
    on Yorkshire 181
Trumper, Victor 75, 78
The Trundlers (Pearson) 69
Tufnell, Phil 68, 142, 218, 303
Tutu, Bishop Desmond 135
28 Days Data (Dobell) 194
Tyers, Alan 207
A Typhoon Called Tyson (Tyson) 55
Tyson, Frank 55

umpires 105–12
Underwood, Derek 65, 104, 167

Vaas, Chaminda 296
van Niekerk, Dane 294
Verity, Hedley 56
Vettori, Daniel 275

W G Grace (Midwinter) 74, 258
Walters, Doug 40, 155, 261, 263
Wardle, Johnny 178
Warne, Shane
    'ball of century' to Gatting 165, 271
    on Buchanan 266
    on England 189
    England crowd and 214
    Haigh on 270
    Healy on his diet 261
    Roebuck on 270
    Samuels on 149
    sledging 144
    spectator's banner 142
    on spin bowling 67
Warner, David 45
Warner, Pelham 15, 75, 200, 235
Warr, John 87
Waugh, Mark 269
Waugh, Steve 170, 222, 268, 269,
    299
Welldon, Bishop of Calcutta 16

"When an Old Cricketer Leaves the
    Crease" (Harper) 310
the wicket 231–8
Wickets, Catches and the Odd Run
    (Bailey) 234
Wigoder, Basil 291
Wilde, Simon 192, 277
Willey, Peter 149
Willis, Bob 49, 164, 206, 312
The Willow Wand (Birley) 219
Wilson, Rockley 199
Wisden
    Cardus on Sobers 89
    Engel on England attitude 188
    Engel on umpiring 109
    Hobbs on Hammond 41
    Marks on Gatting 272
    obituary of Cec Pepper 110
    Pinter on 11
    Robertson-Glasgow on one-day
        cricket 257
    tribute to Hyland 318
Wodehouse, P G 266
women's cricket 174, 176, 177, 286, 289,
    294, 299
Women's World Cup
    1993 286
    2009 289
Woodcock, John 175
Woodfull, Bill 198, 199
Wooldridge, Ian 228, 229, 254
Woolley, Frank 78
Woolmer, Bob 129, 276
World Cup
    1975 35, 53, 249
    1992 223, 225, 229
    1994 187
    1996 187, 188
    1999 289
    2003 228
    2007 288
    2011 193, 291
World Twenty20 64, 192, 287
Wyatt, Woodrow 23

Yallop, Graham 103
Yardley, Bruce 124
yorkers 52, 64
Younis, Waqar 52

Zimmermen (Berkmann) 21